WISE
LIVES

Orthodox Christian Reflections on
The Wisdom of Sirach

by Patrick Henry Reardon

Conciliar Press
Ben Lomond, California

WISE LIVES:
Orthodox Christian Reflections on the Wisdom of Sirach
© Copyright 2009 by Patrick Henry Reardon

Published by   Conciliar Press
                 A division of Conciliar Media Ministries
                 P.O. Box 76
                 Ben Lomond, California 95005-0076

Printed in the United States of America

ISBN 978-0-9822770-3-4

For our beloved Bishop Mark
of the Orthodox Diocese of Toledo

CONTENTS

Introduction

The Wisdom of Sirach is popularly classified among the "apocryphal" books of the Bible. This is not an accurate description, however; the word "apocrypha" means "hidden," in the sense of having doubtful or spurious authorship. In truth, there is nothing even slightly "apocryphal" about the authorship of this book, inasmuch as the author explicitly identifies himself.

He is Joshua ben Eleazar ben Sirach, and, as we shall see in the course of this commentary, it is quite striking how much we are able to learn about this man directly from the book that bears his name. We know, for instance, that Joshua ben Eleazar ben Sirach (hereafter Sirach), inasmuch as he lived and wrote in the early second century before Christ, is among the last authors of the Old Testament.

Although Sirach composed his work in Hebrew, most of the original text is now preserved only in fragments, the largest of which (containing 39:27—44:17) was found at Masada in 1964. That discovery supplemented other extensive fragments discovered in Cairo in the late nineteenth century and among the Dead Sea Scrolls in the 1950s. The original Hebrew of this book, it appears, was the basis for its earliest translations into Syriac.

For the past two thousand years, however, the Christian Church has mainly preserved the entire Greek translation of this book, a translation made by the author's grandson in Egypt sometime after 132 BC. From this Greek version, preserved among the manuscripts of the Septuagint, the Wisdom of Sirach passed into the other translations of the ancient Church: Coptic, Latin, Slavonic, and Arabic. It also appears that the Septuagint influenced the later Syriac versions of the work.

The present commentary is based on the canonical Septuagint version of Sirach, though I have consulted the original Hebrew in the available fragments.

For the purpose of consistency, I generally quote Sirach and other biblical books according to *The Orthodox Study Bible*. When my interpretation of the Sacred Text differs from that translation—which is sometimes the case—this difference is noted, and, when necessary, defended.

THE PERSPECTIVE OF THE BOOK

In general it is true to say that Ben Sirach represents Israel's older, more conservative pursuit of wisdom. He especially cherishes the time-tested truths, the practical lessons derived from antiquity through tradition. Thus, he is not much given to the theoretical speculations, the bold probing of difficult problems, of the sort we find in Qoheleth and Job. Sirach is not disposed to search out matters above his abilities (3:21) or engage in unwarranted curiosities (3:23). Often enough, he believes, pursuits of that sort are largely pretentious (3:25).

For this reason, perhaps, Sirach has sometimes been regarded as excessively pessimistic about human abilities. Herman Melville, for example, speaking for the Protestants, remarked on their rejection of Sirach from the canonical Scriptures: "And, now that I think of it, how well did those learned doctors who rejected for us this whole book of Sirach. I never read anything so calculated to destroy man's confidence in man" (*The Confidence Man*, Chapter 45). A grim assessment, surely. Speaking for myself, nonetheless, I can think of any number of books that accomplish the task of discouragement more effectively than the Wisdom of Sirach. *Moby Dick* comes to mind, for instance, and *Billy Budd*.

While it is true that Sirach entertains no great hopes for men without God's grace, it is not the case that his attitude toward things human is cramped and narrow. Indeed, the very opposite is true. For starters, Sirach is well versed in the literature of his religion, particularly the Torah and the Wisdom books. In addition, he has traveled widely and appreciates the personal enrichment available to the traveler (34:9–11). He especially values the scientific skills of medicine (38:1–8; contrast 2 Chronicles 16:12). Sirach's hymns (42:15—43:33), in addition, testify to both his regard for the wonders of nature and his personal abilities as a poet. This author lived a long time and reflected wisely on the varying fortunes of human life (51:13–22).

While the perspective on wisdom in Sirach resembles Israel's older approach, which is characteristic of the Book of Proverbs, five differences are usefully noted.

First, Proverbs preserves its wisdom sayings in traditional forms derived from a variety of ancient sources. The Book of Proverbs is essentially a compilation from many sources. In Sirach, on the other hand, the various wisdom sayings are distilled through the personal reflections and literary craft of a single teacher and writer. Israel's proverbial literature has been filtered through Sirach's own experience. Thus, in his portrayal of the ideal rabbinical sage (38:24—39:11), Sirach appears to be giving us a description of himself. When he instructs the young man coming to the service of God to prepare his soul for temptation and adversity (2:1–5), he understands whereof he speaks.

Sirach also employs a much larger variety of literary forms. In addition to the proverbs, which provided the name for that earlier work, Sirach includes hymns, prayers, and a long historical meditation. He also makes more specific references to the Torah and the prophets. Indeed, Sirach was, above all, a scribal teacher, who handed on to young men an inherited curriculum that included the Torah, the prophecies (including what today we call the Bible's "historical books"), and the accumulated body of Israel's proverbs and parables (38:34—39:5). This curriculum of wisdom, then, was theological, moral, literary, and historical.

Second, Sirach's perspective on wisdom, by reason of its extensive recourse to history and biography, is less abstract than that of Proverbs. That earlier book consisted largely of apothegms already employed for a long time in a thousand different contexts; well before they reached the Book of Proverbs, those maxims had become general—universalized as it were—losing the personal qualities they may have carried in their original contexts. In principle, Proverbs could have been written at nearly any period of biblical history.

Thus, Proverbs has nothing comparable to the "praise of honored men" which is one of the most remarkable and endearing parts of Sirach (44:1—49:16). In this lengthy section Sirach, setting in review the revelation of God's wisdom in the lives of great men over an extended historical span—from Adam to Nehemiah—gives praise to God for that revelation. Even as he speaks of "praising honored men," it is really God who is given the glory: "The Lord established His great glory / And majesty from the beginning through them" (44:2).

And this, surely, is the proper response to such critics as Melville, who regard man as God's rival and imagine that all glory given to God must work towards man's diminishment. While Sirach ascribes all glory to God, he never uses this ascription to the disparagement of man.

Third, Sirach's interest in biography is of a piece with his more general interest in history. Whereas the wisdom taught in the Book of Proverbs was presented as timeless, Sirach represents a later effort to study Israel's history itself through a "wisdom lens." In this regard the text bears comparison with another late Old Testament book, the Wisdom of Solomon.

Fourth, written after the Book of Job, Sirach's work benefits from the insights of that book. We will reflect on this influence during the course of the present commentary.

Fifth, it is not difficult to discern in Sirach a polemical preoccupation with respect to the Hellenic culture that was threatening the moral standards of Israel at that time. This preoccupation will also receive considerable attention during the course of the commentary.

STYLE

Although the education offered by Sirach was literary, a great deal of the content of this book reflects—and embodies—the vast pre-literary material characteristic of traditional Wisdom literature. That is to say, the maxims and proverbs of Israel had been handed down for centuries by memory, and they were often crafted with a view to memorization. This fact explains why so many of these maxims are binary in construction, whether by antithesis, or synonymous parallelism, or polarity, or merismus, or couplet, or any of several other double formulations. These simple binary forms cause the material to stick more easily in the mind. In his recourse to this rhetorical style, Sirach is of whole cloth with the Bible in general.

SIRACH:
PROLOGUE IN THE SEPTUAGINT

ॐ

Sirach's grandson and translator, who arrived in Egypt in 132 BC, composed this prologue as a kind of *apologia* for the book. He explains that his grandfather had drawn the material from three sources, which we recognize to be the three parts of the Hebrew canon of Holy Scripture: the Torah, the Prophets, and the other books of the Fathers (cf. also Luke 24:27, 44).

Our translator further explains that his effort was intended for the benefit, not only of those to whom the Bible was an inheritance—the Jews—but also for those outside (*tois ektos*) of Israel. He was convinced that the wisdom of this book had a wider application for anyone who truly loved learning (*paideia*).

Christians will see in this intentional effort to make the wisdom of Israel available to the non-Jew a new step in what we venture to call "evangelization." Sirach represents a distinct move to "evangelize" the Gentiles. Two aspects of this effort come to the fore as new:

First, there is the simple phenomenon of translation into a Gentile language, which Sirach's grandson admits was an arduous undertaking. He comments that those who have read the three parts of the Holy Scriptures in Hebrew (*Hebraïsti*) recognize that the translation of these books does not have the same force (*ou gar sodynamei*) as the original. They differ not a little (*ou mikran exei ten diaphoran*), he says.

These translations, like the Aramaic Targums in use in Palestine, were intended for the use of those Jews who could no longer understand Hebrew. Once these were translated, however, those who were not Jews could also read them. The translations, therefore, inevitably became a bridge between Israel and other peoples and cultures.

In this Prologue we find the first evidence of a conscious intention to share the wisdom of Israel with the Gentiles, so that the latter might come to know the Torah and perhaps also to live by the Torah. We are not exaggerating, then, in referring to this enterprise as a new step in the history of evangelization.

A second aspect of this newness is a fresh approach to wisdom: It places this subject explicitly and coherently into the history of salvation.

Unlike Proverbs and Job, which in different ways explore the paths of wisdom with only a passing attention (if any at all) to the Torah and salvation history, in Sirach we detect a deliberate effort to make the Torah and salvation history integral to the pursuit of wisdom. That is to say, we find here in Sirach an endeavor to see Israel's covenants and history fulfilled and perfected in the man of wisdom. His is a wise life.

The wise scribe, then, bringing forth from his treasury both old things and new, is the man that embodies in life and thought a kind of fulfillment of Israel's covenantal history. Such a one embodies the inheritance of Israel, incorporating the Tradition into his own life and philosophy, and thus making it more attractive than the intellectual resources available in other nations and cultures. Such a man transcends the limitations of his own lifetime and becomes part of the greater Israel, whose days are innumerable (37:25). He takes his own place among the "wise lives" of history.

EXCURSUS:
The Book of the Church

The traditional name for this book in Latin is "Ecclesiasticus," literally "The Churchman." Although it was not included among the books of the Hebrew Bible, the early Church seems to have had little or no trouble accepting its canonicity. Indeed, the Church Fathers appeal to it and quote it more frequently than they do many books of the Hebrew Scriptures. Found in virtually all the ancient Christian codices of the Bible (Sinaiticus, Vaticanus, Alexandrinus, and so forth), this is preeminently a "book of the Church."

In three ways, we may say that the Church's

---

incorporation of Sirach into her own canon was an important theological step, which reflected a proper recognition of both the author's historical insight and his "evangelical" effort.

First, Holy Church, interested in the fulfillment of Holy Scripture as an integral component of her evangelism (Luke 24:44–48; 1 Corinthians 15:3–4), appreciated Sirach's historical survey, in which the lives of Israel's heroes embodied God's salvific wisdom. This insight represented an important step toward the fullness of revelation, in which all of biblical history was perceived as fulfilled in the life and work of Jesus of Nazareth. The Church discerned in Sirach's effort an important step toward the fulfillment of biblical history in the proclamation of the Gospel, a proclamation always made "according to the Scriptures."

Second, the Church recognized in Sirach's appeal to the non-Jew an important step in the history of evangelism, the crowning hour of which included the Gentiles in the company of salvation. Those Gentile "fearers of God," who gathered around the synagogues of the Mediterranean world and were the beneficiaries of Sirach's work, became the earliest non-Jews to enter the Christian Church.

Third, the literary work of Sirach was both theological and apologetic, and in both respects it was fulfilled in the proclamation of the Gospel, which itself is both theological and apologetic. That is to say, it has a meaning for both those inside the Church and those outside.

That synthesis of theology and apologetics, crafted by the genius and Spirit-endowed insight of Sirach, was inserted by the Church into the full biblical canon—the larger synthesis created in history by God's incarnate Word and the Holy Spirit.

~: SIRACH 1 :~

The first chapter is thematically divided into three parts: (1) God as the source of wisdom (vv. 1–8), (2) the benefits of wisdom (vv. 9–18), and (3) practical counsel on the discipline necessary to attain wisdom (vv. 19–27).

Sirach begins with the theme of measure; we notice that the verb *arithmeo*, "to count," is found twice (vv. 2, 9). Like classical philosophy in general, the Wisdom literature of the Bible regards measure and proportion as the most readily discernible signs of wisdom.

This truth was first perceived in wise men themselves, those whose judgment could be trusted because they were seen to weigh all considerations, to balance conflicting ideas and interests, and thus to reach decisions proportioned to both justice and fact. The ancient path of wisdom was always associated with due measure and proper proportion. Excess, on the other hand, was universally perceived as the mark of chaos and disorder.

Just as a sound, solid house was recognized in its proportion, order, and distribution, so a sound, disciplined, well-regulated life—a wise life—was discerned in the traits of moderation and due measure.

Measure, on the other hand, was assessed in accepted units, or "numbers" (*arithmoi* in Greek). The acceptance of limits was fundamental to good order, and limitation itself implied mathematics; things are limited by the application of numbers. Indeed, this insight led philosophers like Pythagoras to regard numbers as the basis of reality.

Since the world itself manifests such measurement, Hebrew wise men likewise reasoned that the Creator must provide the source and root of the wisdom He has placed in the structure of the world. He alone discerns the "arithmetic" of things.

This created wisdom, the first of God's works, is identified with the light of intelligibility in which all things were made (v. 4; Genesis 1:3). Yet, Sirach does not regard wisdom as identical with God, but as a creature that is poured out on other creatures (v. 9). Wisdom in this book is always created wisdom, not the consubstantial Wisdom of the New Testament and the Christian faith.

As wise, says Sirach, God is greatly to be feared (*sophos, phoberos sphodra*, v. 8), so the fear of God is man's first step towards wisdom (v. 14). Ironically, however, the fear of the Lord is also the source of man's pleasure and joy (vv. 11–13).

In this chapter's second part (vv. 9–18), Sirach speaks of the advantages of wisdom. We especially note the attention given to "the fear of the Lord," which Sirach describes as wisdom's beginning (*arche,* v. 12), root (*hriza*, v. 18), crown (*stephanos*, v. 16), and fullness (*plesmone*, v. 14). This fear of the Lord is a deep religious reverence. A wise man, therefore, is a devout man, keeping his spirit humble in the sight of God. He spends his life, which itself is God's gift, in the service of God (*doulevein Kyrio*, 2:1). The wisdom begotten of reverence is careful to preserve the proper measure and proportion in life, restricting disordered impulses and holding the passions at bay. This personal restraint pertains thus to the service of God.

In this section the reader is particularly struck by the irony that the "fear of the Lord is glory and boasting" (v. 9). If—as must be the case—the fear of the Lord includes humility, how is it expressed in "boasting"? We gain some grip on this question if we observe that the word for "boasting" here, *kauchema*, has the same root as the verb Paul used when he quoted Jeremiah: "He who boasts, let him glory in the Lord" (1 Corinthians 1:31; Jeremiah 9:24).

In Sirach's context, this assertion about boasting may have to do with his apologetic concern for Israel's sense of self-respect. As the contemporary Books of Maccabees attest, Sirach's fellow countrymen were full of self-doubt in the face of the prevailing pagan culture. Here our author provides them with the symptoms of genuine humility: "glory and boasting"!

The final part of this chapter (vv. 20–29) begins to apply some practical, if general, considerations to the principle that the fear of the Lord is the beginning of wisdom.

In practice, a man starts his quest by controlling his temper (v. 22). This effort requires some measure of courage, insofar as the loss of temper seems to be always somewhat *in fashion*, at least among males. That is to say, since the indulgence of anger is widely perceived as an expression of manliness, it is perhaps more readily accepted in society than certain other, grosser vices, such as mendacity and theft. Indeed, this social acceptability may encourage a man to indulge his wrath rather than curb it.

Its social acceptability, nonetheless, does not render anger less of a hindrance to the quest for wisdom. In this case, as in so many other instances, the indulgent standards of society tend not to favor the pursuit of wisdom. Later on, James (1:19) will exhort a man to be "slow to wrath." Moreover, a man can be destroyed by his own anger. It is driven away, Sirach tells us, by the fear of the Lord.

The opposite of wrath is, of course, patience, but patience, of its nature, requires time to bear fruit in joy (v. 23). This is a lesson our author has learned from his study of Jewish history.

Control of the temper is of a piece with control of the tongue (v. 24); "slow to speak, slow to wrath," as James puts it (1:19). While a man patiently maintains godly silence, he must have something profitable to think about. The proper subject of his reflection will be the traditional maxims (*parabolai*) that transmit wisdom (v. 25). The man who cherishes such reflection is possessed of "reverence" (*theosebeia*), which the sinner does not respect.

Wisdom is God's gift, but it is not accorded to everyone indiscriminately. God gives it to the man who fears Him and observes His commandments (vv. 26–27).

Because the fear of the Lord does not immediately produce success—as men understand success—a person will be tempted to give it less than full allegiance (v. 28). He may give it only half his attention and effort, creating a bad combination of faith and distrust. This is what our author calls a double heart. Such a state will in due course become manifest, because the fear of the Lord cannot be faked very convincingly (vv. 29–30).

EXCURSUS:
The Character and Experience of Sirach

In the Book of Sirach, the pursuit of wisdom has a more personal aspect than is the case in the Bible's other Wisdom books—perhaps even an implicitly autobiographical aspect. We find in the pages of this work a vast accumulation of inherited teaching, but it is distilled in a living, identified soul, taking on a unique and personal form.

We may contrast Sirach, in this respect, with the Book of Proverbs. Even if we think of Solomon as the "implied author" of Proverbs, this supposition tells us next to nothing about Solomon as a person, because the counsel conveyed in Proverbs is intentionally objective, pretty much bled free—as it were—of the author's subjective evaluations. Even the other collections of aphorisms in Proverbs tell us precious little of Agur or Lemuel's mother.

Indeed, this objective, universal quality of the inherited sapiential aphorism represents its strength. The traditional wise man, as represented by . . . well, let's say Bildad the Shuhite, strives to convey timeless truth, inherited obediently from the past. Even when an individual wise man did contribute some new gem to the accumulated inheritance, he did so anonymously. Bildad's moral reasoning, as portrayed in the Book of Job, was uncomplicated. It possessed simple, straightforward answers learned from those who had gone before (Job 8:8). This is precisely the approach we find in the Book of Proverbs.

In Sirach, on the other hand, the ancient aphorisms of Israel's traditional wisdom receive an infusion of the author's own blood. Their objective validity has passed through his existential assessment and experience, thereby taking on—if the expression is allowed—a personal face. Sirach's teaching demonstrates the wise life of the author himself, so that wisdom assumes in these pages what I have proposed to call an autobiographical form.

In other words, readers of Sirach are able to approach this writer rather much as he himself approached the "famous men" examined in the final chapters of this book. We seek in his life what he found in theirs. All wise lives are the embodiment of wisdom.

For this reason, in studying the Book of Sirach, one is prompted to speak of the author's "experience." He certainly seems worthy to be called a "man of experience." Indeed, the idea of "experience" offers an excellent avenue for the study of Sirach.

Prior to considering the experience of Sirach, however, it will be useful to reflect on the various senses in which we use this English noun. For instance, by "experience" we often mean an individual event in which someone is involved, or some particular thing that happens to somebody. Understood in this way, our English "experience" corresponds to the German *Erlebnis*, which can mean "occurrence," "adventure," or "event."

"Experience" in this concrete, existential sense is often pluralized: we say that a person has had various kinds of experiences, which may include education, travel, work, hazards, social settings, unique opportunities, and so on. If we consider a person's sundry experiences cumulatively, we may be disposed to call such a one "experienced." Having passed through many things, he is thought of as "a man of experience." Indeed, among the dictionary's various definitions of "experience" we read, "*the sum total of things* that have happened to an individual and of his or her past thoughts and feelings." Used in this way, the description "experienced" is quantitative.

Sirach can certainly be called "experienced" in a quantitative sense, inasmuch as he exhibits the refinements attendant on advanced education, a breadth of sympathies born of travel and wide exposure to different cultures, a poetic understanding derived from the contemplation of nature, a scientific perspective given by familiarity with technical skills, a patience begotten of suffering, and the mature self-assurance that comes from years of active teaching. In short, Sirach has accumulated many experiences that are brought to bear on his quest of wisdom.

Our English "experience" also has another meaning, however, a special meaning that resists being pluralized. In fact, experience in this second sense cannot be plural, because it is not quantitative. It indicates, rather, the quality of a person (*qualis*), not the number of things (*quantum*) he has been through and learned from. Experience in this qualitative sense, which corresponds to what the Germans call *Erfahrung*, has to do with the formation of the mature human soul. Such a man is experienced not simply in the sense of having had many experiences, but in the sense of being transformed through the activities of his life. He is now a qualitatively different person; his has become a "wise life."

Experience in this second sense contains both moral and intellectual attributes. The "man of experience," considered as a moral being, is possessed of what we call "character," a Greek word meaning "internal shape." The classical notion of character indicates that a man has gradually crafted his soul through persistent adherence to God's Law, the sustained discipline of temperance and proper restraint, assiduous attention to social and moral duty, and the steady determination of right choices made over the course of many years. By the exercise of prudence, justice, courage, and self-control, this man's soul has been rendered ready for God's gift of wisdom. This is the "man of experience" in a moral sense.

As an intellectual quality, this kind of experience is expressed in a greater breadth of perspective, which is the product of many years of reflection, thought, and disciplined study—all of this corresponding to the Greek word *paideia*, usually translated as "training" or "education." The importance of *paideia* in Sirach's mind is suggested by the appearance of this word thirty-six times in his book.

It is essential to reflect that this kind of experience is far more than—and very different from—an accumulation of individual experiences. It is something beyond the harvesting of fruit; it is, rather, the eating and assimilation of that fruit. The gathered fruit is now integral to the man himself.

Understood intellectually, this experience involves the integrative effort of disciplined thinking —even dialectical thinking, by which a man corrects his misunderstandings. It is the product of one's personal informed thought and enlightened interpretation of life. This experience is not abstract but essentially an aspect of history itself. This essential quality of it was well expressed by Hans-Georg Gadamer as "the inner historicity of experience."

The man of experience, as we understand the term here, is largely formed by his choices, but these choices are made within the limitations of specific historical settings—chiefly the person's complex duties toward his society (as a child, a spouse, a parent, a worker, a leader or teacher, and so on) and the deliberate incorporation of the inherited culture that identifies him.

Principal in this latter respect is a man's reflection on the content of his inherited language. Language, which is obviously essential to the formation of ideas, is also necessary to a person's self-consciousness. Because language is essentially social and traditional, a person acquires both his ideas *and* his self-consciousness within his active relationship— through language—to both his contemporaries and his ancestors. In short, both society and tradition, structured by language, are essential to the experience that leads to wisdom and self-knowledge.

Even the most casual reader of Sirach must observe his persistent ethical attention to the duties imposed by language.

We should make one further consideration about experience: The wise man never becomes a "know-it-all." He continues to live and learn. In the words of Gadamer, "Genuine experience [*Erfahrung*] is experience of one's own historicity." Wisdom is almost a verb! It is the continued activity of a wise life.

But to say that experience takes place within history—that it neither seeks nor acquires a non-historical perspective—is to assert that the attaining of wisdom always leaves room for "more." As long as history lasts, the door of experience is never closed. An active openness to the future—a quiet tinge, at least, of prophecy—lies in the heart of a wise life. Perhaps Sirach's readers will gain some sense of his suspicion that the best was yet to come.

ᴄ⁖ SIRACH 2 ⁖ᴐ

This chapter is composed of two sections, each of which is concerned with the most elementary components of wisdom—namely, the fear of the Lord and His faithful service.

The very moving first section (vv. 1–6) is addressed to the young person who represents the "audience" presupposed all through this book. In the first verse we have the first instance of the forty-six times this "child" (*teknon*) is addressed throughout the Wisdom of Sirach. It may be the case that our author has in mind the actual pupils in a rabbinical school under his supervision.

Be that as it may, this term "child" (habitually translated in *The Orthodox Study Bible* as "my son") indicates that the transmission of wisdom is according to age. In other words, the young person is to benefit from the accumulated insight and perspective of the generations to which he is heir (compare Proverbs 1:15; 2:1; 3:1). These earlier generations have already learned, from experience and study, what the neophyte needs to know, and the transmission of this wisdom pertains to his inheritance.

In this first section of the chapter, the author introduces two ideas that were arguably less obvious in the earliest stages of Israel's Wisdom literature. First, wisdom consists in the service of God (*doulevein Kyrio*). Second, the attainment of wisdom is impossible without patience in tribulation. Neither of these themes—inseparable in the mind of Sirach—is so dominant in the earlier perspective represented in the Book of Proverbs.

In fact, rather the opposite was the case. Although the Book of Proverbs had certainly exhorted the young person not to despise the Lord's chastening and correction (Pr 3:11–12), he was also promised that he could expect blessings and other good things if only he kept the traditional rules, applied himself industriously, and avoided occasions of sin.

Here in Sirach, however, the young man is told—upfront!—that his soul will be tried. It is suggested that he is in need of purification, even humiliation (*tapeinosis*, v. 5). While Proverbs did speak of the soul's purification by fire (Pr 17:3; 27:21), Sirach warns against apostasy (*aposteis*) in the face of such trial.

The young person, therefore, must receive an augmented instruction on the subject of temptation. He must learn in detail, not only of the blessings promised to those who endeavor to please God, but also of the trials that will inevitably accompany that effort. He must be informed, at the very beginning, what to expect in this regard.

It is the apparent merit of Sirach that he emphasizes this theme in the traditional exhortation of youth that had always been part of Israel's Wisdom literature. Reading his Proverbs through the lens of Job, Sirach sees that the expected beneficiary of the inherited wisdom must know the whole story. It is not enough to tell the young person that all will go well if only he keeps the rules and brings godly governance into his life. He must also know that the Lord invariably permits His servants to be tried by fire. The pursuit of wisdom will be accompanied by very difficult temptations.

James will be the clear transmitter of this same message to the Christian Church (Jas 1:12). Indeed, James refers to Job with respect to this subject (5:11).

The second part of this chapter (vv. 7–18) has an elaborate rounded construction (called a "chiasmus") with five components, the center one a description of the Lord Himself (v. 11). Each of the five parts of this construction has three elements. This structured section may be outlined as follows:

1—a triple description of "those who fear the Lord" (*hoi phoboumenoi Kyrion*)—verses 7–9

2—three rhetorical questions beginning with "who?" (*tis*)—verse 10

3—a threefold description of the Lord, each component doubled—verse 11

2´—three woes (*ovai*)—verses 12–14

1´—a triple description of "those who fear the Lord" (*hoi phoboumenoi Kyrion*)—verses 15–17

We may now take the five stages of this construction in detail. Three consecutive verses (7–9) exhort those who fear the Lord (*hoi phoboumenoi Kyrion*) to believe on and trust in Him. That is to say, if the fear of the Lord is the beginning of wisdom, its next steps have to do with a patient confidence in God. Wisdom is the gift of God, after all, not simply the fruit of human striving.

The analogies of the farmer and the fisherman are useful here. Both men must work very hard, nor will they gain, without work, what they desire. But in each case the desired benefit is always a gift from on high, and not simply the fruit of their efforts. Both vocations, consequently, require a good deal of waiting and patient trusting. One must not "turn aside" (*enklinete*, v. 7). The fear of the Lord is expressed in "believing" (*pistevsate*, v. 8) and "hope" (*elpisate*, v. 9).

This threefold appeal to those who fear the Lord is followed and matched by three rhetorical questions concerning God's fidelity in times past with respect to those who trusted and waited on His mercy (v. 10). Each question begins with "who?"

These three questions in turn are followed by a triple description of the Lord, each component doubled: "compassionate and merciful," "longsuffering and pitying," "forgiving and saving" (v. 11). These traits of the Lord are the foundation of man's faith and hope.

This triple description of the Lord is followed by three "woes" against those who fail to fear the Lord (vv. 12–14). These woes, which are directed at those who fail in courage and simplicity of heart, correspond to the earlier questions (v. 10) about those who did fear the Lord.

Finally, these three woes are followed by a second description of those who fear the Lord (vv. 15–17). As in the original description, there are, once again, three components. Everything in this second part of the chapter is thus arranged in threes.

These first two chapters of Sirach, then, supply the foundational ideas for the rest of the book: the source and nature of wisdom, and the service of God in His faith and fear.

EXCURSUS:
Sirach and the Book of Job

In making the two themes of chapter 2 (the service of God and patience in trial) central to Israel's "mainline" wisdom transmission, Sirach is apparently the heir of the Book of Job, that thornier of Israel's reflections on wisdom.

The Book of Job, we recall, mounted something of a challenge to the moral motivation pronounced in the Book of Proverbs. Whereas Proverbs had promised divine blessings on the blameless and upright man, who feared God and shunned evil, the Book of Job told a very different story: At the beginning of the Book of Job, the major character appears as the very embodiment of the moral ideal held up in the Book of Proverbs. Yet the entire book goes on to describe the terrible trials and torments to which he was subject in soul, body, and condition.

Here in Sirach we find these ideas from Job incorporated centrally into the traditional instruction given to the young person. Like Job (Job 1:8; 2:3; 42:8), this "child" is called to "serve" God, in which service he can expect to be tried and humiliated, almost beyond measure. This idea Sirach learned from Job—that the true servant of God is a suffering servant.

Indeed, both Sirach and the author of Job seem to have learned this lesson from the very hot furnace of Jewish history. Namely, the lesson that those who would be the Lord's servants in this world—the devoutly humble—can expect trials and further purification. This theme of purification and redemption through suffering became very important, through all the ensuing centuries, to all Jewish reflection on history. We find it as early as a sixth-century editorial hand in the Book of Isaiah, and all the way to a twentieth-century masterpiece called *The Last of the Just*, by André Schwarz-Bart.

Moreover, the earliest Christian reflections on history, beginning with Jesus' identification of Himself with the Suffering Servant of Isaiah (cf. Mark 14:24;

Luke 22:26–28), made this idea the very foundation of soteriology, or the theology of salvation.

❧ Sirach 3 ❧

This chapter has two parts: The first is about a man's relations with his parents (vv. 1–16), the second about humility and gentleness of heart (vv. 17–29). For reasons not entirely clear, Sirach here changes the address to plural—"children" instead of "child."

Since the fear of the Lord is the beginning of wisdom, it is appropriate that the wise man regards first his duties toward God. This was the subject of the two previous chapters.

In the present chapter, however, it is time for the wise man to regard his duties toward his parents, inasmuch as wisdom is part of his inheritance received from those that went before him.

In fact, this is the proper order indicated in the Decalogue, where the honoring of parents follows immediately after the commandments respecting God. Prior to other duties a man owes to the rest of his neighbors, his responsibilities to his parents come immediately after his debt to God. The correct order of wisdom, therefore, first considers our Creator and then considers our procreators. This is the proper sequence in a just and well-ordered life.

So important is this first social duty, the duty toward parents, that the man who fulfills it "atones for his sins" (*exsilakestai hamartias*, v. 3; cf. v. 15).

Although the enunciation of this duty most often mentions the father, it is not adequate to think of it as purely "patriarchal." Indeed, with respect to filial duty, Sacred Writ does not much distinguish between fathers and mothers. Mothers exercise judgment (*krisis*) over sons (v. 2), and a wise man "honors his mother" (*ho doxsazon metera avtou*, v. 4).

Moreover, the wise man knows that such honor given to the past transmits also a treasure to the future (v. 5). That is to say, a wondrously inverted law of reciprocity operates in history, a poetic form, as it were, of the *lex talionis*: What a man sows with respect to his past he will also reap with respect to his future.

This is why the only future blessing specifically mentioned in the Decalogue is attached to the commandment to honor one's parents: "Honor your father and mother *that it may be well with you, and your days may be long* upon the good land the Lord your God is giving you" (Exodus 20:12, emphasis added). Sirach is pleased here to recall this promise (vv. 8–11). St. Paul will make the same point: "'Honor your father and mother,' which is the first commandment with promise: 'that it may be well with you and you may live long on the earth'" (Ephesians 6:3–4).

It is also instructive to recall that all the commandments in the Decalogue are negative in character—prohibitions—except two: the observance of the Sabbath and the honoring of parents. Only for these two subjects did God consider appropriate an affirmative mandate, and not simply a prohibition. Both subjects—the Sabbath and parents—are positive constitutive institutions of the moral universe.

After the Flood, we remember, the first curse was brought on the man who dishonored his parents; that was the one sin, we may say, that survived the drowning of sinful humanity (Genesis 9:20–27). It produced the first curse in the new world. God's attitude on the honoring of parents has not changed (v. 16).

The second part of this chapter is about humility and gentleness of heart (vv. 17–29). These reflections follow logically on the previous discussion about reverence toward one's parents.

If the beginning of wisdom is the fear of the Lord, the beginning of folly is an arrogant view of oneself. It is small wonder, then, that Sirach devotes much attention to the sin of pride (cf. 10:6–18). The peril of pride, in the eyes of Sirach, was one of the proven lessons of history, a lesson amply demonstrated with respect to Egypt, Assyria, Babylonia, Persia, and very recently, Carthage (defeated in 201 BC, the end of the Second Punic War). All of these nations had perished in their pride.

Humility, however, is the proper sentiment of the man who fears the Lord and reverences his parents. He is once again addressed as "son" and told to do everything "with gentleness" (or "meekness," *en prayteti*, v. 17; cf. the same word in Matthew 5:4; 11:29; 21:5). As he grows older and becomes more important (*megas*), the young man must take care to humble himself yet more in the sight of God (v. 19).

The truly dangerous and more damning pride, for Sirach, is

the pride of the intellect. He seems to be warning here of the lofty philosophical speculations that cause a man to seem intelligent—at least to himself—but which inspire nothing better than a pleasant satisfaction with the exercise of his own mind. This is especially the case if the speculator is in over his depth (v. 20). The man that pursues this path will likely neglect his real responsibilities, which often concern humbler matters (v. 21).

The quest of wisdom, then, is not advanced by idle intellectual speculation. It is rooted, rather, in plain things that God has already set out for us in the manifestation of His will.

The immediate danger Sirach has in mind here was posed by the various brands of Hellenic speculation running rampant in the Holy Land at that time, distracting the devout Jew from the study of God's will in the Torah. Those new movements of intellect were producing a new kind of Jew, one who prided himself on his "progressive" views. Indeed, this intellectual pride posed even a political danger, which this book's Greek translator had recently witnessed in the Maccabean crisis.

Intellectual pride is perceived in the inordinate attachment of a man to his own opinions (v. 23), and it is the mission of wisdom to set men free from this attachment. Folly of this sort is not safe; it will destroy the soul.

The humility recommended by Sirach is inseparable from reverence. It is "devout" humility, humility born of the fear of the Lord, the only sort of humility sponsored in Holy Scripture. It is the cultivated attitude of the mind that lives in God's presence—the heart in the presence of the Burning Bush. If a man entertains a humble view of himself, this view is the progeny of his reverence in the sight of God.

Such a man prays,

Lord, my heart is not haughty,
Nor my eyes lofty.
Neither do I concern myself with great matters,
Nor with things too profound for me.
Surely I have calmed and quieted my soul,
Like a weaned child with his mother;
Like a weaned child *is* my soul within me.

O Israel, hope in the Lord
From this time forth and forever.
(Psalm 130 [131], author's translation)

✑ SIRACH 4 ✑

As we have seen in Sirach already, the true pursuit of wisdom does not isolate the human being from the rest of society. Biblical wisdom, far from being an elitist quest, strengthens a man's bonds to all human needs and aspirations. Even an eremitical character like Elijah, after all, showed himself supremely at one with his fellowmen and entirely concerned with their well-being.

Indeed, any philosophical endeavor that isolates a human mind from other human minds—or a human heart from other human hearts—moves directly at variance with the true quest of wisdom. Biblical wisdom is to be found, not in man's separation from others, but in a man's common continuity with the human race—including the human race that went before him and will come after him. That is to say, the true quest of wisdom socializes a man, not only in the present world, but also in respect to the past and the future.

So far in this work we have considered this socializing aspect of wisdom in two respects. First, the desire for wisdom prompts the humble man to respect his parents, who form his original, most radical link with history and the human race (3:1–16). Second, the love of wisdom discourages a man from isolating his mind in the cultivation of lofty theories that serve only to heighten his sense of superiority over others (3:17–23).

In the first part of the present chapter (vv. 1–10), we come to a third aspect of wisdom's socializing influence: the cultivated and sustained sense of compassion with respect to human suffering and need. The "child" (v. 1, *teknon*, a term always replaced by the formal expression "son" in the OSB) is exhorted to relieve human suffering as soon as possible. He is encouraged to let the sufferings of his fellowmen enter his own soul and prompt him to attend to them. He is not to harden his heart by passing judgment on the needy, much less to harden the hearts of the helpless by despising their helplessness. It is not the wise man's task to teach patience to those in pain (vv. 1–5). Above all, he must not provoke bitterness in another human soul (v. 6).

Because the poor are also powerless, other men will be tempted to defraud them of personal respect. The wise man will not succumb to that damnable temptation (v. 8). He will become, instead, the advocate of those oppressed at the hands of the powerful (v. 9), and God's love will reward the man who lives this way (v. 10).

We should remark, in this regard, that solicitude for the poor is one of the features of biblical wisdom (cf. Tobit, Job 29, etc.) that most clearly distinguish it from Greek philosophy.

The first steps along the path of wisdom, then, are not strictly intellectual. No mind will rise superior to the heart that supports and sustains it. Before a man learns the rules of logic, therefore, and the skills of critical thinking, he must first train his heart in the habits of reverence, humility, and compassion.

After treating the initial steps along the path of wisdom, the teacher discerns it is now time for the beginner to receive encouragement to continue the pursuit. This encouragement is the intent of the second part of this chapter (vv. 11–19).

Such encouragement is necessary, Sirach believes, because the student may soon feel himself overwhelmed with a host of diverse moral instructions, so numerous and pressing that he may become despondent. Prior to that undertaking, consequently, the teacher determines to discourse on the blessings and rewards of discipline (vv. 11–19), in order to provide the beginner with a clear point of focus and hope. Our author will make this effort of encouragement from time to time, lest the student lose his way in a maze of moral precepts. The next such concentration on the blessings of wisdom will come in 6:18–37.

Sirach describes wisdom as a mother that exalts her children (v. 11), a metaphor perhaps suggested to him by the previous verse, which had spoken of a mother's love (v. 10). Long traditional in Israel's sapiential literature, this feminine imagery for wisdom continues through verse 19.

Mother Wisdom, far from being elusive or remaining aloof, comes in pursuit of those that seek her (v. 11). She is described less in terms of knowledge than of love. This is a spiritual love, *agapan* (twice in v. 12, twice more in v. 14).

The man who obeys wisdom is raised to universal knowledge, able to perceive the lessons of history. This is what it means to "judge the nations" (*krinei ethne*, v. 15). The wise man, if he adheres obediently to wisdom, is given the discernment to survey with understanding the rise and fall of empires. He will seize by wisdom the patterns and meaning of history. Sirach will provide a lengthy reflection on such discernment in chapters 44—50.

In this promise to the seeker of wisdom, the Book of Sirach touches Israel's tradition of prophecy, because it was the whole business of prophecy to discern and proclaim the significance of historical events and the destiny revealed in the patterns of those events, even as they unfolded. The wisdom that instructed the sage is the same as that which inspired the prophet. This is the wisdom handed down through Israel's "generations" ("posterity," OSB; *geneai*, v. 16).

Although this historical understanding is the inheritance of God's people, it is not handed to each person on a silver platter, free of charge. Wisdom must first try and purify a man. He must learn, through his own experience of suffering, what history has taught Israel through centuries of suffering. Through this suffering and dereliction, however, wisdom will walk with him (*porevsetai met' avtou*, v. 17).

In this description of wisdom's leading we recognize once again the figure of Job (Jas 5:11; Heb 12:3–11).

The final goal, nonetheless, is not absolutely assured. If a man abandons wisdom, wisdom will abandon him (v. 19). As long as a man still breathes, he is capable of failing!

Next begin some simple, practical applications of the pursuit of wisdom, applications that will last for several chapters. The final section of this chapter (vv. 20–31) explores the first of these applications.

The student of wisdom is taught (according to the KJV) to "keep watch for opportunity." In the transmitted Greek text, this is a rich expression: *syntereson kairon* (v. 20).

To grasp the significance of this counsel, we recall that the Greek language has two different words for time: *chronos* (from which we have "chronic" and "chronology"), which designates time in sequence, or "the flow of time"; and *kairos*, meaning an instance of time, an occasion, time as the moment, the "now."

The young man is exhorted to keep watch over this latter kind of time, the moment in which he is living and of which he is conscious, the only kind of time over which the human being has some measure of control, the moment that allows and offers a decision or a choice to be made.

This guardianship of the moment is an important component of the psychology of Sirach, indicating a special active consciousness and moral self-awareness. We may contrast this sense of *kairos* with a half-consciousness dominated by *chronos*, time as fluid, what in literary criticism is known as "the stream of consciousness." Immersed in the flow of time, the mind "goes with the flow." It rushes on in the current, unable to determine its destiny.

Sirach will have none of this. The student of wisdom is to safeguard the occasion, observe the *kairos*, exercise stewardship over the moment, and impose a moral form on the present. Preserving himself from evil, he must not be ashamed to take control of his soul (v. 20).

As a specific application of this ascetical effort, the student of wisdom must guard his relations with others, so that no one is able to shame him into doing evil. He must show no one a respect that involves the compromise or sale of his soul (vv. 21–22).

There follows a series of exhortations about speech. The pursuer of wisdom must not hold his tongue on those occasions when by speaking he may do good (vv. 23–24); this is an example of the proper stewardship of *kairos*.

But the wise man must never speak in a way that compromises truth, nor be afraid to confess either his ignorance (v. 25) or his sins (v. 26). On the other hand, he must also know when to back off and not use violence against the inevitable (v. 26). The good tongue is the tongue under control, and speech is no substitute for deeds (v. 29). It is useless to impress a fool with one's own understanding or to fawn before the powerful (v. 27).

A man's lifelong struggle—a "fight to the death" (*heos thanatou agonisai*)—is the pursuit of truth, and God Himself will do battle on behalf of such a man (v. 28).

With respect to the domestic life, a man should recall that no one enjoys living in a lion's cage (v. 30). He must not, through bad temper and an uncontrolled tongue, make life in his home unpleasant. Outside of his home, moreover, a man should know when to keep his hand open and when closed (v. 31).

⌒: SIRACH 5 :⌒

This chapter, which is made up mainly of a series of negative exhortations ("Do not . . ."), is particularly concerned with the spiritual dangers of arrogant presumption (vv. 1–9) and the importance of self-restraint (vv. 9–15).

The overly presumptuous crowd usually includes a lot of young people. Their native sense of strength and vitality makes it easy for the young to exaggerate their self-confidence. All too often, indeed, this self-confidence is fortified by subsequent successes in life. Because a man may live and succeed for a long time before life teaches him otherwise, he may wander down a path of self-deception for much of his lifetime. Hence, the teacher of wisdom instructs him early regarding the dangers of excessive self-reliance.

The young man is warned against too much confidence in what he owns or controls (v. 1), against placing excessive trust in his own ideas and the promptings of his own heart (v. 2), against an arrogance born of success (v. 3), and against an unrepentant mind that tries God's patience (v. 4). All of these things betoken a false security, about which the inexperienced need instruction.

Above all, a man must not presume to imagine that the divine punishment is less real for being delayed (vv. 5–6). Caution is required here. Man must not put off his repentance simply because God has postponed his punishment (v. 7).

This is particularly the case when a man's "success" in life is the result of robbing others, whether by defrauding them of property or depriving them of opportunity (v. 8). Sirach knows very well that some men have risen by standing on the prostrate necks of those less fortunate.

In the second part of this chapter (vv. 9–15), Sirach returns to the social nature of wisdom, which demands self-restraint. A man chiefly attains the habit of self-control in his discourse and relations with other men, exercising control of his tongue (vv. 9–10, 13) and temper (v. 11), sharing with others the knowledge derived from his study and experience (v. 12), and avoiding duplicity in all things

(v. 14). Since human institutions and all relationships among men are founded on mutual trust, a special malice attaches to the man whose speech is deceitful. Sirach calls him "double-tongued," *diglossos* (vv. 9, 14; 6:1).

In all these matters we discern Sirach's view of the wise man as an active participant in the life of society. He is not a solitary thinker and theorist. His wisdom is manifest, rather, in his godly competence in the world of men—the economic world, where human beings earn a living for themselves and their families; the political world that fosters the happiness of communities and the well-being of nations; and the social world, where nearly every enterprise rests on the trust human beings place in one another. This world of society is the true arena of wisdom.

~: SIRACH 6 :~

Two large subjects divide this chapter: *philia* and *paideia*, friendship (vv. 1–17) and education (vv. 18–37).

Sirach starts with friendship, about which he arguably has more to say than any other biblical writer (cf. also 9:10–16; 19:13–17; 22:19–26; 27:16–21; 37:1–6). We do not know if Sirach espoused some metaphysical theory on the nature of friendship or some psychological explanation of why we need it, because he never speaks of these things. He gives us, rather, a series of practical counsels about how to encourage and maintain friendship.

From time to time, I will argue that Sirach's stress on friendship is rooted in his appreciation of the social nature of wisdom. As we reflected in the previous chapter, Sirach's pursuit of wisdom is always related to the essentially social structure of the human soul.

The basic task, our author says, is to strive to be a "friend" (*philos*, v. 1), because the cohesion of society abides in friendship, the necessary condition of which is personal and institutional trust.

The extreme opposite of a friend is what the Bible calls an *echthros*. In the present context this word, normally translated as "enemy," perhaps may be rendered as "sociopath"—the arrogant, insensitive individual, not to be trusted, someone unable to treat others as friends. He is a habitual backbiter, devoid of sympathy, and quick to altercation. Such a one corresponds pretty closely to what Holy Scripture calls a "fool."

The near cousin to this man is the person who entertains too lofty a view of himself, fostering an attitude of personal superiority that others will distrust and find offensive (vv. 2–4). A real friend, in contrast, will be pleasant of speech and easy of approach (v. 5).

This latter quality prompts Sirach to mention the caution required in the choice of a confidant and counselor among one's friends. "One in a thousand" is his rule of thumb (vv. 6–13).

There is no theoretical flourish in this advice. Experience has proved many times that relatively few friends are blessed with the prudence to be confidants or the steadfastness of character to be supportive in the hour of trial. One can love his friends but still withhold from them what he knows to be information beyond their ability to manage. Christ our Lord loved those men of whom the Evangelist wrote, "But Jesus did not commit Himself to them, because He knew all *men*, and had no need that anyone should testify of man, for He knew what was in man" (John 2:24–25).

A man enjoying his prosperity may find that he is surrounded by many friends, but he must exercise vigilance over what he entrusts to them. Some of these fair-weather friends may turn on him when his season of prosperity has ended, and he will be the more vulnerable for having been incautious in his confidences.

What a man most wants to see in his friend is the fear of the Lord, because this is the most reliable guarantor of their friendship. If a man is not the friend of God, he is not safely chosen to be the friend of anyone else (vv. 16–17).

The chapter's second half (vv. 18–37) deals with *paideia*, a very rich concept that includes both instruction and discipline. "Education" is perhaps our best translation of *paideia*.

This expression from classical Greek culture appealed very much to the emerging rabbinical tradition of late Judaism. *Paideia* appears 28 times in the Septuagint version of Proverbs, most often to translate the Hebrew *musar*, "discipline." Sirach speaks of *paideia* 36 times and uses the verbal form, *paidevo*, 15 times. It means, "to educate," a concept much richer than simply "to teach."

Wisdom, as a habit and an internal principle, is not normally available to the young. Rather, it becomes a habit and an internal principle only after years spent in the restraint of the passions, the fostering of a virtuous life, instruction in the inherited understanding of the Tradition, and the study of God's Law. In the attainment of wisdom, then, maturity is normally and generally an essential factor.

What *is* available to the young is *paideia*—instruction, education, training, discipline. If the young man continues to cultivate discipline and seek instruction, says Sirach, in his old age he will attain to *sophia*, wisdom. The one is the reliable path to the other (v. 18), very much as plowing and sowing construct the path to the harvest (v. 19).

Sirach admits that this is bad news for those who want quick and easy results (v. 20). These will experience instruction and discipline as oppressive, as though a heavy stone were crushing them (v. 21).

Discipline is something to which we *submit*, says Sirach (v. 23). He even compares it to a chain (v. 24). Who willingly submits to wearing a chain? Only the man who knows his need to be under control, the man who is sincerely afraid of hurting either himself or others. A chain is, after all, an instrument of control, and in the present context it is an instrument of *self*-control.

Jesus uses the metaphor of the yoke to much the same effect: "Take My yoke upon you and learn from Me" (Matthew 11:29). This is essentially the same invitation that we have in Sirach. The yoke, light as it is, is still a yoke; it is an instrument of control; it is something to be borne in order to learn: "Take My yoke upon you and *learn* from Me."

In bearing the yoke, of course, we in due time find "rest" (*anapavsis*, v. 28). The same idea appears also from the lips of Jesus in the same context: "you will find rest [*anapavsis*] for your souls." The identical promise is found in both places—the bearing of the yoke leads in due course to the "rest" of wisdom.

At this end, Sirach says, the chains of discipline become the insignia of honor (vv. 29–31).

The path to wisdom is through the discipline of hearing and paying attention (vv. 32–33, 35). Generally speaking, it does not come from talking but from listening. The young man must seek out someone to instruct him (vv. 34, 36).

Above all, he must pursue the study and observance of the Torah, the commandments of God (v. 37). This emphasis on the Torah is the aspect of biblical *paideia* that most separates it from classical Greek culture.

ᔓ Sirach 7 ᔓ

The idea is currently widespread that public life obliges its participants, at least on occasion, to do things that are evil. This idea is especially prevalent in the areas of politics and economics, where a highly competitive spirit gives rise to the impression that, in order to succeed against the competition, a certain cutting of moral corners is at least condoned.

In various business endeavors, for example, it is often presumed—and sometimes said explicitly—that a general atmosphere of dishonesty requires some recourse to duplicitous practices, shady deals, and deceptive policies. In certain situations, it seems, men are expected nowadays to lie and deceive. It becomes almost part of a game, as though there were no strict moral distinction between, say, stealing a checkbook and stealing second base.

A like attitude can be found in politics, where it is often assumed that men can rarely be taken at their word. If such is the case in politics, it is even more so in geopolitics, because relatively few men feel deep loyalties beyond their own borders. Nations are presumed not to trust one another, which is the reason they spy on one another. This is also why they subject one another's spies to torture.

The dishonesty so common in the realms of economics and politics easily spreads, however, to other areas of public life, such as recreation and education. Thus, athletes have been known to cheat in competition as readily as students cheat on exams.

In all such instances, we observe a certain moral nonchalance with respect to public life, as though the public life were outside the moral sphere. Indeed, it is very often said that morality is a private matter.

In Holy Scripture, however, no such distinction is made. The same moral principles pertain to both aspects of life, starting with the simple rule, "do no evil" (v. 1). In fact, in the Bible the quest of goodness is a public pursuit, not an individual partiality. The moral law is a public law, not a private preference.

In the judgment of Holy Scripture, then, those who flout the moral law create moral chaos in society. They lower the moral atmospheric pressure and bring about an unhealthy moral climate, whether this is done by a lying politician, a scandalous movie star, a shady businessman, or an athlete on steroids.

It is really the case, however, that we all know this, no matter what we say to the contrary. At the basis of all public law lies a deep moral law that provides a public standard. This is why we employ policemen and maintain a standing army. These institutions are not simply an assertion of will; they are expressions of moral intellect.

Sirach deals with this matter in the present chapter, which is concerned with social and domestic sins.

First among the social evils to be avoided is, according to Sirach, the ridicule of the afflicted (v. 11). No man's soul is to be embittered by personal derision, especially the taunting of a personal defect.

A second social evil to be avoided is mendacity. Because all of social life is based on the bonds of trust, a person who lies is unfit to live in society (v. 12). To lie about others is an especially heinous crime, because the person who does it cuts deeply into the social fabric, which covers the nakedness of us all. Such a person is worse than the man who poisons wells.

A third social evil to be avoided is that of simply shooting off one's mouth in the presence of those who are older and more experienced. Worse than that, moreover, is shooting off one's mouth in the presence of God. Both sins, symptomatic of arrogance (v. 14), are incompatible with humility of soul—*tapeinoson sphodra ten psychen sou* (v. 17). Only the man with a humble soul is the person fit to live in society.

A fourth social evil to be eschewed is the betrayal of a friendship for the sake of advantage or gain (v. 18). Such a betrayal is among the worst of sins. Indeed, we recall that the selling out of a friend was the sin of Judas Iscariot. It was concerning that sin that we are told it would be better for a man never to have been born.

A most serious extension of the sin of personal betrayal is the betrayal of a spouse (v. 19). If the bonds of loyalty hold all of social life together, this principle especially applies to the bond of marriage. It is the betrayal of this bond that brings about the destruction of families, which are the most basic and indispensable components of social life. The man who betrays his family is a special kind of Judas.

Sirach's next admonitions (vv. 20–36), which pertain mainly to domestic life, are plain and down-to-earth. Indeed, the reader may feel there is little about these admonitions that he would not know on his own. He may wonder how he would not already know—even without being told so in the Bible—that a man must not oppress his servants (vv. 20–21), must take good care of his livestock (v. 22), must discipline his children (v. 23), must keep a close watch over the behavior of his daughters and marry them to good husbands (vv. 24–25), must be faithful to his wife (v. 26), must honor and care for his parents (vv. 27–28), must reverence and support the clergy (vv. 29–31), see to the well-being of the poor (v. 32), care for the burial of the dead and the consolation of the bereaved (vv. 33–34), and visit the sick (v. 35). Any morally upright person, any decent citizen of any cultured society, knows these things to pertain to his moral responsibilities. Why does the Bible even need to speak about them?

In posing this question—to which the answer seems obvious—we touch on one of the notable characteristics of biblical wisdom: namely, the Bible's Wisdom literature, including the present book, is where Holy Scripture enters into conversation with the moral and philosophical traditions of humanity in general.

The Bible's Wisdom tradition did not arise in a social vacuum. From the very beginning, in the most primitive parts of the Book of Proverbs, the Bible's teaching on wisdom took account of the sapiential traditions of Egypt and Babylon. Many of the Bible's wisdom-sayings, the proverbs and basic domestic instructions, have their parallels in the moral teachings of ancient peoples, and these contacts grew through the centuries. The moral traditions of mankind are the intended audience of the Bible's Wisdom literature.

In this sense the Wisdom books of the Bible offer humanity its easiest access to the vast wealth of Holy Scripture. Even those with no faith in the God of the Bible may feel an innate sense of the truth of the Bible's Wisdom teaching, because this teaching is addressed to the common moral sense of the human race. It is the meeting place where the Bible converses with the moral logic of mankind.

↝ Sirach 8 ↜

This chapter has two parts, of which the first (vv. 1–9) deals with prudence, and the second (vv. 10–19) treats of what—for want of a better term—we will call privacy.

First, there is prudence (vv. 1–9). In the pursuit of wisdom, one begins with the most elementary kind of prudence, the sort needed for bare survival. Now it is obvious, with respect to survival, that most of us are provided with limited resources. All of us were born naked and not terribly far from utter starvation, and, during the entire course of our lives, few of us live very far from disaster at any given moment.

Most of us are not very powerful, rich, or especially influential. Indeed, as St. Paul observed, there are not many of us wise according to the flesh, not many mighty, not many noble. On the whole, in short, we are provided with rather limited resources in life.

Since we find ourselves in a world where others are wealthier, wiser, and more powerful than ourselves, we must find and guard our way, just as a matter of survival. This is why we are obliged to develop the habit of practical prudence. Happily, it is in the cultivation of this necessary habit that we commence the great quest of wisdom. Although wisdom involves a great deal more than common prudence, it will never be attained without common prudence.

Consequently, among the most elementary admonitions of biblical wisdom we find warning against doing imprudent things. These warnings include counsel against provoking the powerful (v. 1), cautions against taking on battles we can't win (v. 2), advice against inciting those who are given to anger (v. 3), and injunctions against stirring the discourteous impulses of the coarse and ill-bred (v. 4).

These are very basic bits of counsel. They are not absolute, obviously, because adherence to moral principle may require us, on occasion, to provoke the powerful, to take on battles we can't win, to risk the anger of those who oppose us, and to hazard our chances with those who are rude. Still, unless adherence to a higher moral principle requires otherwise, simple prudence will prompt us to be careful in these matters.

Such basic prudence will also urge us to honor the aged (v. 6), to respect the dead—even in the case of our dead enemies (v. 7), to learn from those more experienced than ourselves (v. 8), and to attend to the inherited understanding that has proved itself through many generations (v. 9).

We rather often hear that the young only learn from their mistakes. If this were the case, of course, there would be no such thing as education. Every generation would be obliged to figure out life as though no one had ever done so before. It is simply not true that learning from one's mistakes is the best way—much less the only way—to learn. On the contrary, learning from one's mistakes is the harshest, most expensive, and least efficient way to learn. The very effort, in fact, sometimes precludes survival.

It is far better to learn in such a way as to *avoid* mistakes, profiting from the simple rules, inherited admonitions, and successful examples of those who have gone before us. Prudence, then, urges us to learn from the *past*. Hence the importance of moral tradition.

The second part of this chapter (vv. 10–19) encourages what we may call a kind of privacy. This privacy is expressed by a sense of wariness in the presence of possible danger, especially danger from people who do not inspire confidence. The ability to discern such people pertains to elementary prudence, which was the subject of the chapter's first half.

There is a dilemma here: Because trust is the necessary foundation of the social order and all social life, we may be tempted to imagine that there should be no limits to trust. That is to say, if trust is a good thing, how can there be too much of it?

There are two objections to be raised against such a line of thinking, the first objection *a priori* (that is, on the basis of a logical principle), and the second *a posteriori* (that is, on the basis of experience, human testimony, and accumulated knowledge).

First, the thesis that "there is no such thing as too much trust" is objectionable *a priori*, because it involves a distorted perspective. It shifts a qualitative observation to a quantitative point of view. To imagine that no limits are to be placed on any created good is to remove that good from the realm of quality to that of quantity. It is like saying that if a Chihuahua is a good dog, a Chihuahua weighing 75 pounds is much better.

The notion of the "good" is clearly qualitative, which is to say that it involves conformity to some standard. The notion of the good does not invoke the question "how much" but "of what sort?" In a dog show, when two Chihuahuas are compared to determine which is the better one, this comparison presupposes some kind of standard, some idea of what would be the perfect Chihuahua, the ideal of Chihuahuahood.

We all admit, I suppose, that a nose is a good thing. We all recognize, as well, that the goodness of the nose is not the sort of premise that leads to the inference, "a bigger nose is a better thing." "The bigger, the better" is not a useful principle in the evaluation of noses.

In all created goods, there is measure and proportion, and this principle pertains to that good called "trust." There can be too much trust for the same reason that there can be too much nose. Trust, like all things finite, must conform to a proper standard of measure, and this proper standard is to be determined, I believe, by experience.

We come, then, to our second objection to unlimited trust. It is not warranted *a posteriori*: it is not supported by our experience. In the second half of this chapter, Sirach lists some examples in this experience.

Sirach tells us that human experience, as handed down through the ages (v. 9), cautions us not to place confidence in sinners (vv. 10–11), to be wary about committing ourselves to those who are powerful (v. 12), not to oblige ourselves beyond our abilities (v. 13), to recognize situations that exceed the limits of our control (v. 14), to avoid the company of those who are recklessly bold (v. 15), to put distance between ourselves and those given to anger (v. 16), and not to share our thoughts with those unworthy of our confidence (vv. 17–19).

The second half of this chapter, then, completes the first half. The prudent recognition of our limits prompts us to consider well the limitations of others, and to guide our lives accordingly.

~: SIRACH 9 :~

Sirach has little to say to the recluse. It is the implied supposition of this book, rather, that the pursuit of wisdom is normally conducted within the field of active society, within the moving processes that make up the economic, political, and cultural life of the human community. The wise man, for Sirach, is not disengaged from social life. He is, on the contrary, a willing and active participant in the normal interests and endeavors of the social order. He does not attain wisdom in spite of this social engagement, but in and through it.

As we had occasion to reflect in the previous chapter, the studious application of prudence in this social engagement accomplishes two things. First, by drawing attention to the reality of human limitations, it prevents a man from making serious and destructive mistakes in his dealings with other human beings. Second, his studious application of prudence and discernment gives shape to his first steps toward the final attainment of wisdom.

As we have also reflected, the application of prudence is most often expressed in simple restraint, especially the control of the passions and the curbing of the tongue. The man who would attain unto wisdom sets a close watch over his emotions and his impulse to speak.

This is a hard thing for modern man to hear, because he is influenced by certain worldly biases, which include a preference for spontaneity with respect to the passions and a sympathy for self-expression with regard to the tongue. Hence, conscientious restraint over the passions and restrictions on self-expression are burdens that do not sit lightly on modern man.

Yet, as we have seen, in the Wisdom literature of Holy Scripture such exercises of discipline are absolutely essential to both the social order and the attainment of wisdom. Neither is feasible without what Irving Babbitt called "the inner check," which means the freely assumed self-censorship of the serious and disciplined man.

The first part of the present chapter (vv. 1–9) turns this perspective toward what is perhaps its most obvious field of application: the sexual difference that divides—but also unites—human beings. It is in the field of sexuality that a wise society constructs its highest walls and exercises its closest supervision, because sex is arguably the most dangerous force on earth. Like electricity, sex carries the potential for great good, but also like electricity it involves a constant risk, requiring a sustained control and circumspection.

In the present chapter this control is expressed in a series of emphatically negative formulations—a list of things one must *not* do. Repeatedly Sirach tells his readers, "do not be jealous" (v. 1), "do not give your soul to a woman" (v. 2), "do not meet with a woman who is a courtesan" (v. 3), "do not associate with a dancing-girl" (v. 4), "do not gaze at a virgin" (v. 5), "do not give your soul to prostitutes" (v. 6), "do not look around in the streets of a city" (v. 7), "do not gaze at beauty belonging to another" (v. 8), "never dine with another man's wife" (v. 9). There is at least one "don't" in each of these nine verses.

Any person with even a modest experience of life knows and understands the necessity of these prohibitions. The problem is that human beings begin to feel the erotic impulse long before they are mature enough to understand it. They are like little children fascinated with matches or electricity. They are disposed to experiment.

Sirach's rules, however, are not just for the young. In some individuals the allurements of sex remain strong even unto old age, so it has happened that many men and women, having lived chastely and soberly in their earlier lives, succumb to this temptation in later years—much to their embarrassment and the humiliation of their grandchildren! These verses of Sirach, then, are intended for lifelong application. One does not "outgrow" them.

The second half of this chapter (vv. 10–18) contains practical exhortations, mostly of a cautionary sort. Once again, there are indications of what kinds of people are to be avoided.

For example, we are told to put distance between ourselves and those who may cause us harm (v. 13). This very practical counsel may help us to determine, for instance, what sort of neighborhood we may choose to live in, because we don't want to place ourselves and our families in physical danger. Holy Scripture very simply says, "Stay away from dangerous people." This is not subtle advice.

These sundry exhortations touch not only our outward conduct, but also our inward dispositions. Thus, we are told not to take interest in the activities of the ungodly, remembering the Lord's judgment on those activities (v. 12). This bit of counsel would seem to preclude, among other things, the pursuit of magazines and other publications devoted chiefly to gossip about the doings and lifestyles of entertainment celebrities. Such a pursuit is at best a waste of time, but often enough it lowers our moral sensibilities as well.

This section likewise contains a winsome analogy between the skilled craftsman and the wise ruler (v. 17). Just as the first is experienced in the use of his hands with tools and the material on which he is working, so the second has mastered the gift of language and the use of it to govern his fellow men. This image testifies to the classical thesis that proper governing is born of the persuasive power of speech that is both rational and rhetorically attractive. Sirach presents us with a high view of government. He says that rational human beings are to be ruled by adult persuasion, not by coercion and the imposition of will.

Perhaps the most attractive verse in this section is the one that compares old friends to old wine (v. 10). The simile is simple: as wine improves with age, so does friendship. So, if friendship is wisely cultivated, it is often the case that our best friendships are with those with whom we have been friends the longest.

In this assertion we grasp something of the Bible's practical spirit. It is not a pragmatism that directs all activity to the attainment of further goals. It does not inculcate the idea that all activity must "go somewhere." On the contrary, some activities are not supposed to go anywhere. Some human activities are goals in themselves, needing no further justification. Among these are the activities that contribute to simple friendship. Friends are not there for our use. Friendship is a very good thing in itself, requiring no further purpose or justification.

❧ SIRACH 10 ❧

This chapter has two parts, the first (vv. 1–18) devoted to the theme of governance, and the second (vv. 19–31) to the fear of the Lord.

The Wisdom books of the Bible, including this one, profess a special relevance to those placed in authority, who bear specific responsibility for the well-being of others, whether as heads of households, elders in a community, or leaders of nations. The manner in which such men meet their responsibilities leaves its moral mark on those for whom it is exercised, whether unto good or evil. Simply by his example, a bad ruler will corrupt his people (v. 3), much as a bad father will corrupt his children.

This means that governance in any society serves also a pedagogical function. A ruler teaches the governed by the way he governs, whether in a family, a community, or a nation. A good ruler must be not only efficient ("get the job done"), but also . . . well, "good." This is why character is always pertinent and important in the choice of political leaders.

From this consideration of governance (vv. 1–3), Sirach goes on to reflect that God governs all things (vv. 4–5). If that is the case, then all men, but especially those charged with special social responsibilities, must take care lest they unwittingly (to say nothing of intentionally!) attempt to replace the governance of God. They will avoid vengeance (v. 6), for example, and covetousness (v. 9), but especially pride (v. 7). Pride is what brings nations low.

Indeed, Sirach refers to what today's politics would call a "regime change" (v. 8). He may have in mind the recent rise of the Seleucids over the Ptolemies in the governance of the Holy Land. Kings will also die, he reminds the rulers of the world (vv. 10–11), so pride is always unwarranted.

Pride begins when a man turns his thoughts away from God (v. 12). When this happens, he replaces God in his intentions and begins to assume God's role in his activities.

History testifies to the dramatic consequences of this alteration. In the instances cited by Sirach (vv. 13–17), we may discern the plagues visited upon Egypt (Exodus 7—11), as well as other instances closer to his own time: the fall of Nineveh in 612 BC, the conquering of Babylon in 539 BC, the defeat of the Persians at Gaugamela in 331 BC, the death of Alexander in 323 BC, and the recent fall of Carthage to the Romans in 201 BC. All of these historical examples testify to the folly of pride (v. 18), and it is to history that Sirach sends us to learn this serious moral lesson.

In the second half of this chapter (vv. 19–31)—and by way of contrast to the glory pursued by pride—Sirach speaks of the true glory the Lord bestows on the humble and God-fearing. He speaks of the fear of God five times (vv. 19, 20, 21, 22, 24).

Love for God, far from being contrasted with the fear of God, seems more nearly identical with it; the one is called the seed and the other the plant. Both are expressed in the observance of the Torah (v. 19).

Hebrews 11:7 says that Noah, when he built the ark, was "moved with godly fear." This was a healthy fear. Noah's contemporaries, on the other hand, were fearless. What did it gain them? The fear of God is a good and salvific thing, and in Noah's case, according to Hebrews, it expressed his faith.

Whatever a man's social standing, then, the fear of the Lord is the proper glory of it (v. 22). Indeed, a certain caution is necessary, lest we take a man's social status too seriously (cf. James 1:9; 2:1–4). Wisdom is often enough found among the poor.

This emphasis of Sirach lays a serious qualification on the ancient view that the cultivation of wisdom leads to wealth. This altered perspective may come from Job's influence on Sirach, of which we spoke earlier.

In any case, the fear of the Lord, which can certainly be culti-vated by a poor man, surpasses all the honor men themselves are able to bestow (v. 24). It can be found in the wise servant, who will be recognized by the one he serves (v. 25). At the same time, wisdom is different from cleverness; the latter can lead to boasting (v. 26).

True self-respect is expressed in meekness (*en praüteti*, v. 28), not in arrogance and boasting. Sirach's persuasion on this point pertains to a man's integrity, a quality prompting him to respect his own soul (v. 29). Boasting betrays a serious lack of self-respect. The merely social difference between poverty and wealth (vv. 29–31) is quite secondary to this consideration.

⌒: SIRACH 11 :⌒

Sirach continues the theme of true glory by insisting that it is not always obvious nor readily perceived. True glory does not consist in outward appearances, though men are frequently deceived by appearances.

Who would think, for example, that the little bee would amount to very much (v. 3)? It is just a winged insect, much like a wasp or hornet, which it resembles somewhat in appearance and more especially in attitude. Saint Augustine remarked that the bee, in physical appearance, was rather close to the fly—*res erat proxima* (*Tractatus in Joannem* 1.14).

Yet that man would be grievously deceived who imagined the bee to be just another small but dangerous insect. In respect to man's life in this world, it would be difficult to exaggerate the importance of the bee. It is arguable that the bee is more necessary to man's physical existence than any other animal. Although it may not be much to look at, the bee plays a crucial role in the economy of nations.

Indeed, if the bee should suddenly disappear from this world, millions of people would die of starvation, because of all the plants pollinated by the activity of bees. The bee, then, is valuable beyond reckoning, and those who judge things by mere appearances would make a great mistake in despising the bee.

The truth, that is to say, is not found in appearances; this is a demonstrable fact known to all wise people since the dawn of history.

Yet some people still walk the earth who judge all or most things by appearances. Moreover, they make the major decisions of their lives on the basis of appearances. They even choose their spouses and their careers on that basis.

Such folk have learned nothing from history, perhaps because they have not bothered with history, imagining that their own lives are the only ones worth thinking about or caring for. Basing their judgments on how things appear, they continue to make the same mistakes as fools have done in all previous generations.

To such as these, Sirach calls out, "Do not praise a man for his good looks, and do not detest one because of his appearance. . . . Do not boast about your fine clothes" (vv. 2, 4). In short, things are rarely as they appear. Everything must be explored more deeply (v. 7).

Once again addressing the youngster—the *teknon*, "child" or "son"—the wise man exhorts him not to become overly extended (v. 10). This is very common and useful counsel, especially for the young, whose inexperience does not tell them the dangers incurred by attempting too many things at once.

Such over-involvement, says Sirach, will lead to a loss of innocence. It is worth remarking—though Sirach does not mention it—that this loss of innocence usually comes from a loss of perspective. Inexperienced people, commonly unfamiliar with the relative worth of various activities, are often enough unacquainted with the relationships between causes and effects. They are disposed to confuse interest with ability, prone to mistake adrenalin for zeal, and ready to substitute enthusiasm for competence. They are insensitive to their own limitations on all these points.

Such folk don't exactly *lose* perspective; they have never *acquired* perspective in the first place. In a fairly short time, therefore, they find themselves delinquent in their responsibilities and perhaps morally compromised in their sympathies and decisions. Even in old age, some of us still bear the scars of such unwise activities in our youth.

It is a documentable fact that the overextended person is frequently obliged to rush what he does, and therefore often does it poorly, all the while being bothered by the remembrance of things he has left undone (v. 11). It is arguable that most mistakes made in this world are spawned of the conjunction of inexperience with overextension. Often these mistakes can be remedied, but occasionally the harm is permanent.

An antidote for the vice of overextension, Sirach suggests, is the remembrance that all things come from God (vv. 12–15). Man is ever the recipient of blessing, not its initiator. Even the inexperienced person can be the child of grace (v. 17).

These reflections pertain to Sirach's larger teaching on the importance of modesty. A truly modest person is not likely to fall prey to overextension. A truly modest person is not forever trying to *prove* something. Consequently, he is free to ask and receive the blessings of God.

To the man who prospers in godliness (v. 17) is contrasted the one who gains wealth by shrewdness and a miserly spirit (v. 18). There is something truly sad about this latter, who spends his entire life preparing for a future he will not have (v. 19). His situation is pathetic, of course, because he seriously misplaces his hope. Wealth can keep away many evils, but it cannot keep away death, and death ultimately robs a man of what he has devoted his whole life to acquire.

In the Gospel of Luke, Jesus devoted at least one parable to this very theme: "The ground of a certain rich man yielded plentifully. And he thought within himself, saying, 'What shall I do, since I have no room to store my crops?' So he said, 'I will do this: I will pull down my barns and build greater, and there I will store all my crops and my goods. And I will say to my soul, "Soul, you have many goods laid up for many years; take your ease; eat, drink, and be merry."' But God said to him, 'Fool! This night your soul will be required of you; then whose will those things be which you have provided?'" (Luke 12:16–20)

There is nothing especially "spiritual" or otherworldly about this simple truth. It is available to anyone sufficiently observant and reflective to perceive it. It requires no great spiritual insight or mystic vision to discern the irony of placing one's ultimate hope on wealth, for the simple reason that all of us die. It should not be all that hard, therefore, to avoid the deception of wealth.

Nonetheless, men *do* find it hard, because all of us are disposed to ignore and avoid truths that are unpleasant, and death is certainly an unpleasant truth.

Consequently, this parable of Jesus is introduced by a double warning: "Take heed and beware of covetousness, for one's life does not consist in the abundance of the things he possesses" (Luke 12:15).

The tragedy of the miser, in both Sirach and Luke, is not that he dies, but that he dies without really having lived. He has spent all his days in slavery to wealth, and at the end death takes everything away from him. Jesus calls this man a "fool" (Luke 12:20). He can read a ledger, but he has no insight into life itself, because he has been taken in by the deceptiveness of wealth.

ᴄ: Sɪʀᴀᴄʜ 12 :ᴡ

These next two chapters have to do with a man's choice of friends.

At first some of these exhortations about friendship seem rather severe in tone. Indeed, few places in Holy Scripture are more at variance with certain modern prejudices about "getting along" with others.

Our currently prevailing non-judgmental prejudice encourages us to treat all men equally, without reference to their moral character. This modern prejudice is evidenced chiefly among the young, who have not yet, perhaps, experienced sufficient disappointment through an unwise choice of friends.

The great danger of choosing friendship with immoral people is that of lowering one's own moral standards. After all, it is difficult to be unreservedly friendly with someone whose moral standards are notably at odds with one's own. Consequently, frequent association with immoral people will often prompt a person—perhaps unconsciously—to ignore or compromise his own moral standards in order to suit those of his "friend." This reaction is very common nowadays.

For instance, I have lost count of the occasions on which someone has told me that homosexual behavior must not be immoral, because such-and-such a homosexual is clearly a "good person." What such an assessment usually means is that the person has learned to get along with a homosexual individual, so that he no longer regards the behavior itself as reprehensible. If one can get along with and befriend an active homosexual, this becomes irrefutable evidence—as it were—that there is nothing wrong with homosexual behavior.

This form of argument, however, is no more valid than its equal application to a murderer or a bank robber. If murder and bank robbery are out of consideration, a murderer or a bank robber might conceivably be considered a "good person" (kind, loving, self-sacrificing, even generous to the poor). It is obvious, however, that to befriend a murderer or a bank robber on such a basis puts a person at some moral risk: He may—in strict logic—conclude that murder and bank robbery must not be as bad as is generally supposed, because such "good people" can be found in the ranks of murderers and bank robbers.

In such a case—which, I have mentioned, is rather frequent—friendly and undisciplined association with sinners can corrode a person's moral perception and sensitivity. It is in this sense that we should understand the common adage that a man's moral character is best discerned in his choice of friends.

It is a simple matter of observation that many men have been ruined by their choice of friends. Our prisons are full of folk who fell in with the wrong crowd. Those who are unwise in their friendships will lose their reputations, their wealth, and sometimes their lives.

Once again, these simple observations do not require any great spiritual insight, and the moral exhortations in this chapter of Sirach are common to all great traditions of moral philosophy. Adherence to exhortations such as these will not conduct a man to high sanctity, of course, but it will certainly improve the quality of his life and his chances of happiness.

That is to say, if taken seriously, the exhortations in this chapter may spare a man a great deal of trouble. They may keep him out of jail or bankruptcy court. They may guard his reputation and preserve him from disgrace. They may save his marriage. In short, they may make his life happier, which is no insignificant thing.

Among the stewardships for which we must give account, the stewardship of friendship is not the least. Every friendship is an investment, and Sirach warns us to invest wisely.

ᐱ Sirach 13 ᐳ

This chapter continues the theme of caution with respect to friend-ships. It begins by comparing the vicious man to a hot, sticky pitch, which we touch only at the sure risk of our defilement. The message is plain: There are certain types of people that a wise man does best to avoid.

Sirach puts the wealthy in this category, nor is it hard to see why. Common experience testifies to the spiritual dangers often attendant on associations with the rich.

One danger is this: Those that are not rich may be overly impressed by wealth. In the presence of wealth, those not accustomed to it may become morally disoriented, and in that moral disorienta-tion they are tempted to compromise, perhaps even on a point of principle. That is to say, they fall too much under the influence of wealth, thereby forgetting themselves and their own convictions.

Few people, after all, are so impressed by the power of wealth as the poorer man to whom it is unfamiliar. For such a man, the pres-ence of wealth places him in a strange circumstance. He is analogous to a man on a journey to a foreign place, and most travelers, if they are spiritually sensitive, recognize the special force of various temp-tations while traveling abroad. The poorer man in the presence of wealth is similarly placed in spiritual danger. He may sell his soul without being completely aware of it (v. 2). A wise man will accept the limitations imposed by his poverty (vv. 5–7).

The spiritual peril attendant on association with wealth may not be obvious at first (v. 8), because of the elation occasioned by that association. The man who succumbs to that elation, however, especially deserves the name "fool."

Moreover, it is a simple fact of observation that a wealthy man is able to make more mistakes—without adverse consequences—than a poor man can (v. 3; 8:2; 10:30). The wealth of the wealthy man often buys him a certain measure of immunity from harm brought on by his indiscretions. Thus, the poor man is more vulnerable than a wealthy man, a fact that the poor man cannot prudently overlook.

Poorer people generally know this to be the case, but a young poor man may not perceive it right away. He may suffer greater harm from his association with his wealthy young friends. They will go off to college, while he goes off to jail.

As in all points of this book, the spiritual danger discussed here is far more tempting to the young, whose inexperience renders them unable to perceive the dangers of association with wealth.

Because the modest man, in his embarrassment and discomfort, will especially be disposed to speak overmuch when in the presence of the wealthy, Sirach particularly warns against the disclosure of secrets (vv. 11–12). In the presence of wealth it is important to speak little and think much (v. 13). Caution and discernment are mainly needed, and the unfailing possession of one's own soul (vv. 9–10).

Sirach goes to the animal world to illustrate the differences among men. In that world it is common that some animals prey on others, the wolf on the lamb, for instance (v. 17). So, says Sirach, the unequal allotment of wealth and power creates analogous divisions in human society, where some men enjoy a predatory advantage over others (vv. 18–20).

These remarks are descriptive, of course, not prescriptive. Sirach does not applaud nor approve such divisions among men. Indeed, it is obvious that he disapproves of them.

Very often, however, the true and practical moral problem for the wise man is not to remake society according to higher moral standards, but rather to devise a way to live morally in an immoral world during the brief sojourn of his life on this earth. That is to say, wisdom includes the ability to be virtuous and prudent in a world where the dominant conditions of life lie largely outside of one's own control. Those conditions include the social, economic, and political inequities among men.

Sirach, then, counsels his readers to avoid, as far as possible, the disadvantages attendant on those social inequities, particularly the problems brought about by unwise and unwarranted friendships. There is virtually nothing the lamb can do to remedy his disadvantage with respect to the wolf. He is best advised, consequently, to avoid the wolf's company.

At the same time, our author refuses to condemn wealth, which he insists is not evil in itself (v. 24). In this positive attitude toward wealth we recognize in Sirach the heir of Israel's earlier tradition of wisdom, as recorded in the Book of Proverbs. No reader of Proverbs can conclude that wealth is to be avoided. Indeed, many of the proverbs in that book are specifically directed to the acquisition and retention of wealth.

Sirach writes, however, at a later time, when wealth in the Holy Land was less evenly proportioned, and the cautious tenor of his counsel reflects that financial inequity. That counsel seems directly applicable to our own day.

Having spoken of the dangers of cultivating friendship with the wealthy, Sirach will devote the next chapter to the use of wealth.

~: SIRACH 14 :~

Having warned of the spiritual dangers attendant on association with the wealthy, Sirach now goes on, in the first part of this chapter, to address the wise man's attitude toward wealth itself (vv. 1–19).

The chief danger of association with the wealthy does not come from the wealth as such. Nowhere in Holy Scripture, in fact, do we find a negative attitude toward prosperity in itself.

The danger springs, rather, from fallen man's innate attitude toward wealth. One of the fruits of Adam's sin is a disposition in human beings to worship whatever is good, to confuse the gift with the Giver, and thus to short-circuit the Absolute. Wealth is not the problem; man's disposition to idolatry is the problem. Wealth is only the occasion of sin, not its cause. Wealth, therefore, is dangerous only because greed, like lust and pride, is buried deep in the human heart. The disordered heart is the source of man's problem with wealth.

Consequently, the circumspection that Sirach commends towards association with the rich will remove the occasion of temptation, but it will not, by itself, address the source of the spiritual problem. This problem must be attacked directly. There is need for a change of heart. Even the poorest man in the world can be a miser. Hence, Sirach commends generosity as the only known cure for a stingy heart.

A greedy man is recognized by an insatiable appetite. To such a man there is no such thing as "enough" (v. 9).

Like many wise men who have contemplated the dangers of riches, Sirach exhorts his readers to the remembrance of death, which will put the value of wealth plainly in perspective (v. 12).

It is important, therefore, to use wealth, of whatever size, to do good and to act generously (v. 13), because death is the end of the opportunity for these things. Time, like wealth, is a limited resource, so the earlier one begins to act generously, the better chance he has of not being too late (v. 14). No matter when it comes, death is quite final with respect to time. It always shows up too soon (vv. 15–19).

The closing eight verses (20–27) of this chapter are an exhortation to the persistent quest of wisdom. In order to persevere in that quest it is useful for a man to know, in advance, the blessings that await him. Hence Sirach will speak of the blessings of wisdom.

The man that hears this message must also know, however, that the quest of wisdom will be difficult at first. It will be a matter of "concern" or "care"—"Blessed is the man who will take care [*meletesei;* OSB, "practice"] in wisdom." This verb suggests vigilance and perhaps a touch of anxiety. The path to wisdom requires spiritual effort (v. 20).

This effort is intellectual as well as moral, involving a rigorous discipline of the mind. The second half of that same verse speaks of the "blessed man" as someone who *en synesei avtou dialechthese-tai*—"discourses with insight." One may recognize in this verb, *dia-lechthesetai*, the root of the English word "dialectics," which suggests that the first steps towards wisdom include the cultivation of orderly and disciplined thinking.

This proper exercise of the mind does not, by itself, teach wisdom—for only God can teach wisdom—but it does teach something important and useful. Although one does not arrive at wisdom simply by thinking, wisdom does shed some measure of light on the man who thinks clearly. Such a man will at least be taking steps in the right direction.

What he studies at first will not be wisdom as such but only the "paths" or "ways" (*hodous*) to wisdom. These paths are discerned in his heart (*en kardia avtou,* v. 21). After all, there are paths that lead to wisdom, and there are paths that don't. At many steps on his quest for wisdom, therefore, a man will be faced with new junctures, side roads that make themselves look like the main highway. Indeed, these side roads are sometimes disguised to look like the path to wisdom. The traveler must constantly be making choices. The path to wisdom, therefore, involves a process of consistent and sustained choosing. Hence the need for discernment and prudence.

Bit by bit, however, the man of spiritual discernment comes closer to wisdom. Toward the end of this section Sirach's verbs begin to change his emphasis from questing to abiding. Wisdom is now spoken of in terms of dwelling, not traveling (vv. 24–27). This is the goal of the quest—*abiding* in wisdom.

~: SIRACH 15 :~

Sirach continues to count the blessings of wisdom. In these first verses (1–10) he virtually identifies wisdom with the understanding of the Torah. Practical wisdom, in turn, is pretty much identical with the observance of the Torah. That is to say, the path to wisdom is a matter of obedience to the wisdom of the Torah.

The author regards this identification as a source of comfort, because it means that the young and inexperienced person, who is far from attaining wisdom, can still live a wise life, even before he arrives at wisdom itself. Moreover, he will already be regarded by others as a wise person, simply because they perceive the traces of wisdom in his life.

In fact, living wisely is the true path to wisdom, because biblical wisdom is a practical, not a speculative, thing. It has to do with how a man lives. As a good Jew, Sirach already knows how a man is supposed to live. It is spelled out in the Torah. The Torah, therefore, is the source of wisdom.

A Christian reading of Sirach will take special note of this identification of wisdom and the Torah, because the Christian faith regards God's Son as both Wisdom Incarnate and the fulfillment of the Torah. In everything that Sirach says about wisdom and the Torah, therefore, the Christian reader will see the personal message addressed to his life in Christ. Whatever is said about the Torah is said about Jesus. Whatever is asserted of wisdom is ascribed to Christ.

The second part of this chapter (vv. 11–20) considers man's moral responsibility, which precludes his blaming God for his lot in life. The difference between wise men and fools is a division made by human choice. Indeed, right from Deuteronomy man is faced with the explicit moral choice: "Behold, this day I set before you two paths."

Here in Sirach (vv. 11–12) we see the fool's denial of this choice. He pretends that he is as God made him. He is not responsible for his life.

Sirach will countenance no such evasions, because God does not violate human freedom (vv. 14–16). Just as in Deuteronomy, the choice of life or death is man's to make (v. 17). The very existence of God's commandments bears testimony to God's respect for human freedom.

~: SIRACH 16 :~

Having insisted, in the previous chapter, on man's responsibility for his choices, Sirach now draws the proper inference with respect to bad choices. Men do not want to hear about this subject, of course, but it is a fact that sin does not go unpunished.

The argument for this thesis is not only logical; it is also empirical: history itself bears witness to it. Sirach goes to history to consider examples of *unwise* lives.

Cited first among the empirical examples of the punishment of sin is the fire that devoured the ungodly (v. 6), as it was described in Numbers 16. This story tells of the rebellion of Korah, Dathan, and Abiram.

Sirach then goes on to speak of the evil in the world at the time of Noah (v. 7), when the Flood destroyed the human race. Thus, in the first two examples, we have destruction by both fire and flood.

Next, Sirach speaks of the destruction of Sodom in Genesis 19. We observe that he saw pride—rather than perverted lust—as the defining sin of Sodom (v. 8). Sodom's other sins were the result of pride. Apparently it was Sodom's pride that refused to see evil in perverted sex.

Next, Sirach recalls the six hundred thousand rebels that perished in the wilderness after the Exodus (v. 10). This story, recorded in Numbers 11, is also explained in 1 Corinthians 10.

Our author treats next of the punishment of Pharaoh (v. 15), who was afflicted with the ten plagues and suffered the loss of his whole army at the Red Sea. The worst punishment of Pharaoh, however, was the loss of his moral sense, the hardening of his heart.

Sirach goes on to remark that no man can escape his moral responsibilities by getting lost in the crowd. Numbers do not confuse the divine judgment. There is no such thing as moral anonymity (v. 17).

In the first part of this chapter, then, we perceive two things essential to the formation of the moral conscience. First, Sirach appeals to a detailed familiarity with history as an important source of moral instruction. No man's life, after all, is entirely new. History will teach him much of what he needs to know, as Sirach demonstrates by the examples he cites.

Second, moral responsibility cannot be escaped. God knows all things and reads all hearts.

The last part of this chapter (vv. 18–30) introduces a short treatise on God's wisdom manifest in Creation and history (16:18—17:18). Sirach begins with a meditation on the first five days of Creation (vv. 25–30).

❧ SIRACH 17 ❧

The author now arrives at the sixth day of Creation, and here slows down to consider the human being in greater detail. Indeed, what he has to say about the construction of the human being is a condition for understanding what he has already said about the creation in its lower forms.

Man has been made from the earth, he tells us (v. 1), but in the likeness of God (v. 3). In these two assertions—as in the rest of what he goes on to say about the creation of man—Sirach relies on both of the first two chapters of Genesis.

It is clear in this text that Sirach is not considering man as he was formed in the state of innocence. Otherwise he would not have written of the shortness of man's life and his return to the dust (v. 2). He has in mind, rather, the human state as it has actually been transmitted through history, of which St. Paul wrote, "Sin reigned in death" (Rom. 5:21).

Man's likeness to God has something to do with his dominion over other living things (v. 4). This dominion is based on man's unique ability to think rationally, to reflect critically, and to give creative narrative shape to the contents of his memory and imagination (vv. 5–6).

God's initial revelation to man comes in the form of man's reflective mind, whereby God confers on him an innate moral sense (v. 7) and the rational impulse to regard creation as revelatory of divine truth and glory (v. 8).

God has set His eye on the human heart, so that this heart knows that it is being observed. When a human being truly discovers his heart, he knows that the heart is already being watched by Someone Else. Indeed, man does not really discover his heart except as the object of the divine scrutiny.

This awareness of standing under the divine gaze is the precondition of faith, which is the primal channel of man's communion with God: "Without faith *it is* impossible to please *Him*" (Heb. 11:6).

This divine gaze is the source of man's sense of order and meaning in the world: "By faith we understand that the worlds were framed by the word of God, so that the things which are seen were not made of things which are visible" (Heb. 11:3). This divine gaze into the human heart enables man to behold the wisdom of God at the heart of all things, giving structure and purpose to all that is (v. 9).

Sirach will next go on to speak of God's revelation in human history (vv. 11–18), but first he has been obliged to reflect on what makes human history possible. Human history is not just another dimension of "natural history," because the human being represents a radical disruption in the processes of nature. This radical disruption comes in God's endowment of the human soul with the radical capacity for history. Because he can reflect critically on his experience, employing his ability to arrive at universal principles and make abstract analogies, the human being is the only creature on earth of whom we can say that he has a history.

More specifically, the author cannot go on to speak of God's Self-revelation in history until he has established that principle, innate in man, by which God's historical revelation can be recognized. That is to say, what God does in history cannot be known as revelation unless God first confers on the human heart an impulse toward narrative, a capacity to recall in story form, an innate disposition to review the human experience in a structured account. In other words, there is no such thing as human history unless God first places in man the impulse towards historiography. Man can have a history because God created man as a storyteller.

Before taking up Sirach's reflection on God's revelation at the Exodus, we should reflect on the continuity of God's revelation in nature and in history. This continuity, characteristic of the Bible as a whole, is clearly espoused here in the Wisdom of Sirach.

The continuity of this revelation excludes what we may call a deistic view of Creation, because it includes not only the recognition of intelligent design in nature (which even the Deist sees), but also the perception of intelligent design in history. This latter is obviously much more complex and subtle. Indeed, it cannot be recognized apart from faith.

In the structure of nature, after all, the observer recognizes only one will at work—the will of the Creator. In history, on the other hand, there are many wills at work, God's will and the individual wills of His rational creatures. The wills of men are what cause history; the will of God is what gives it a structured governance.

It is not surprising that many men, while recognizing the intelligent design in Creation, refuse to believe that there is an intelligent design in history. The latter is, after all, far from obvious. History tends to look rather chaotic, and the various philosophies of history not only fail to persuade; they are manifestly at serious odds with one another.

On the other hand, some philosophers, anxious to preserve the divine hegemony over history, refuse to believe that the human will, in making historical decisions, is really endowed with freedom. They speculate that human beings, while pretending to be free in their choices, are in reality only the agents of a larger, more encompassing will, by which history is given direction. According to them, history is really no more complex than nature itself.

Tolstoy, for instance, makes this argument repeatedly in *War and Peace*. We may describe this theory as a sort of move from Deism to Theism, but it still falls very short of a biblical view, which regards both nature and history as the media for God's revelation.

We come next to Sirach's reflections on the Exodus event and Mount Sinai (vv. 11–18). From his pondering on Creation, and especially the creation of the human being (vv. 1–10), he comes to consider God's revelation on the mountain of the covenant. That is to say, he moves from Genesis to Exodus.

In his thoughts on the creation of man, Sirach dwelt in detail on God's placing of a moral sense in the human heart. By reason of God's eye on man's heart (v. 8), the human being has an innate need and native desire for instruction with respect to moral truth (v. 7). This desire is as natural to man's soul as food is to his body. As he needs bread, man requires this instruction in the truth of righteousness.

It was to meet this deep need of the human heart that God spoke on Mount Sinai. Having placed in man's spiritual constitution this appetite for moral instruction, God provided the bread to feed it, because man does not live by bread alone, but by every word that proceeds from the mouth of God. We recall that it was in reference to the encounter on Mount Sinai that Holy Scripture declared that foundational theological principle.

Mount Sinai was the answer to the question God put in the

human heart. Having created in man's heart a need and appetite for the revelatory Word, God came with fire and heat to Mount Sinai to bake, as in an oven, the necessary bread.

By conferring His Torah as a gift to Israel, the Lord took an initial step to redeem mankind from the moral confusions (v. 16) and ethnic divisions (v. 17) that were tearing mankind apart. By inscribing His Law in stone, He preserved the human heart from turning to stone.

It was Israel's vocation to receive on Mount Sinai that revelation needful to the human heart—the moral structure of created existence. God's mysterious choice of Israel was a blessing for the whole human race. Already on Mount Sinai there was implied the law that governs history—namely, that salvation is of the Jews. In Genesis God made all of humanity in His likeness. In Exodus He chose Israel, by a special covenant, to restore that likeness.

❧ SIRACH 18 ❧

The material in this chapter is divided among three subjects. The first (vv. 1–14) is a consideration of God's power and mercy, the second (vv. 15–29) is an argument for prudence in all things, and the third (vv. 30–33) is an introduction to the theme of self-control, a subject that will continue through the following chapter.

In the first part of this chapter (vv. 1–13), the ever-living God (*Ho Zon eis ton aiona*, v. 1) is contrasted with the human being, who will count himself fortunate to live a mere hundred years (v. 9). Indeed, even a thousand years amounts to no more than a drop of water compared with the sea (v. 10).

Although the Lord is marvelous in all the works of His governance and providence (vv. 3–6), He is most to be revered for His mercy "upon all flesh" (vv. 11–14). Sirach, in detecting the divine mercy at the heart of all God's work, is indebted to the Psalmist (e.g., Psalm 135 [136]).

This divine mercy is especially directed to human beings, whose very weakness and sinfulness elicits God's compassion. In this respect, God is likened to a shepherd tending a wayward flock (v. 13; Matthew 9:35–38; Mark 6:34).

God's mercy is shown to man chiefly as He reproves, trains, and teaches him (*elenchon kai paidevon kai didaskon*, v. 13). His mercy is on the man who receives discipline—*paideia* (v. 14).

In the second part of this chapter (vv. 15–29), Sirach once again addresses the young person, the *teknon* (v. 15), in an exhortation to prudence and due restraint, especially in speech (vv. 16–19). Various aspects of personal conduct are considered, with special emphasis on kindness, humility, and repentance from sin. All these concerns are properly assessed if one bears in mind the divine judgment, which every man must face in due course (vv. 22, 24, 25).

Particularly to be noted is the circumspection required as a preparation for prayer; Sirach is conscious of a danger of tempting God in one's prayer (v. 23). He may have in mind the spiritual peril of making rash promises to God (cf. Judges 11:29–40).

The final part of this chapter (vv. 30–33) introduces a longer section on self-control. These verses warn against compliance with one's baser and sinful dispositions to lust (vv. 30–31), riotous living (v. 32), and financial irresponsibility (v. 33).

∾ SIRACH 19 ∾

The practical counsel of this chapter covers three themes: the importance of self-control (vv. 1–5, a subject continued from the previous chapter), the appropriate use of speech (vv. 6–16), and the signs by which to distinguish true wisdom from its counterfeits (vv. 17–30).

The exhortation to self-control appeals to a man's basic self-interest: Loss of self-control is bad for you! Experience proves, for instance, that a drunkard's life is full of misery (v. 1), that illicit sexual indulgence is invariably disastrous (vv. 2–3), that an unwise investment is money wasted (v. 4), and that the approval of evil brings condemnation (v. 5). The avoidance of these things requires no motivation beyond a healthy self-interest.

More to be governed, however, is integrity of speech, the subject of the second part of this chapter (vv. 6–16). When a neighbor's reputation is at stake, extreme circumspection is the rule (vv. 7–8), if only to avoid gaining an enemy (v. 9). Silence in dubious matters rarely causes harm (vv. 10–11).

On the other hand, a proper concern for one's neighbor may prompt a prudent man to speak directly to that person, just to make sure one is in possession of the truth (vv. 13–15).

In the end, nonetheless, Sirach admits most of us have, at one time or another, given offense in our speech (v. 16). The tongue is the last of our organs to be properly controlled.

The final part of this chapter (vv. 17–30) indicates the identifying signs of wisdom, so as not to confuse it with mere cleverness. These signs are chiefly religious, because the fear of the Lord is the beginning of wisdom (vv. 17–20). Wisdom is more moral than intellectual (v. 24).

The counterfeits of wisdom are subtleties in the service of injustice (v. 25), pompous gravity posing as moral seriousness (v. 26), duplicitous appeals to ignorance (v. 27), and moral posturing based on nothing more than not having an opportunity for sin (v. 28)!

Notwithstanding these counterfeits based on mere appearance, says Sirach, one should not conclude that appearances are inconsequential. For example, we should expect that a wise man will not behave like a buffoon (vv. 29–30).

After more exhortations with respect to the tongue, Sirach inserts a series of moral and practical paradoxes (vv. 8–17). Indeed, the pursuit of wisdom can gain no small profit from an appreciation for the phenomenon of paradox. This word, which literally means "beyond appearance," mainly suggests situations of irony and indicates that life is not simple or reducible to easy formulas.

On the contrary, wise men have repeatedly insisted that things are not always as they appear. It is often necessary to go beyond appearances, sometimes even contrary to appearances.

For example, Sirach mentions that good fortune is not always what it seems. It is sometimes ill fortune disguised as an advantage. Contrariwise, what appears to be a tragedy may in fact be a blessing. He writes, "There may be good fortune for a man in adversity, and a windfall may result in a loss" (v. 8).

Perhaps the operative part of the word "paradox" is the prefix *para*, which means "beyond," and the example given by Sirach indicates why this may be the case. Judging by appearances, a good fortune should always be taken for a good fortune, and a tragedy must be regarded invariably as a tragedy. It is the "beyond," however, that will prove the worth and meaning of a thing.

This fact of experience will not be obvious to the young and inexperienced, for the simple reason that their lives do not yet possess a sufficient measure of "beyond." The young have relatively little to look back on, so it is not easy for them to see beyond appearances. Thus, something is taken at face value, even when five minutes of critical reflection would expose it to be something quite different.

In order to appreciate paradox, a person must have a certain accumulation of experiences to give him a sense of "beyond." He must have cultivated some practice at looking back on things, seeing them from the other side, regarding them in the past. That is to say, the acquisition of a "past" is a requirement for the acquisition of wisdom.

A person thus blessed is able to look on his own personal

history and reassess his experiences on the basis of their results. Like Sirach, he will learn that "There is a gift that will not profit you, / And there is a gift where the repayment is double" (v. 10). Perhaps when he first received these gifts, a man thought them both equal. One, however, turned out to be worthless, the other to be worth double its apparent value.

Similarly, something bought cheaply sometimes turns out to be enormously expensive in the long run (v. 12). A humiliating event, likewise, may prove to be a source of personal glory, and vice-versa (v. 11).

This appreciation of paradox pertains also to the assessment we make of other people. Observed closely, a man we took for a friend may turn out to be less than we thought him. An apparently generous man may prove to be deeply avaricious (vv. 14–16).

In order to acquire the "past" necessary to gain a "beyond," it is necessary that a person learn to take his time. That is to say, he must learn not to decide precipitously, not to jump at every appearance of either good or evil, and not to make rash decisions on the basis of inadequate information. A man must somehow learn to look "beyond."

~ SIRACH 21 ~

According to Sirach, the one that "keeps the Law of the Lord gains the understanding of it" (v. 11).

This sort of statement is offensive to modern tastes, because modern man would prefer to reverse the process. He dislikes being told to do something that he does not understand, and here is Sirach boldly telling him that he won't understand it unless he obeys it!

The problem with the modern approach is that it undermines the very concept of obedience. When a modern man says, "Explain it to my satisfaction, and I will obey it," he obeys only his own mind. He is not submitting his will to an authority outside himself (such as the authority of God or the binding address of history). He is, rather, replacing authority with persuasion, demanding, "Convince me, and I will do it." Even if he finishes by obeying, he is just as self-willed as he was before, because he has made himself the authority of his obedience.

For Sirach, on the contrary, understanding of the Torah is not the condition for keeping the Torah; it is the *result* of keeping the Torah. The Torah, after all, is addressed, not to man's reason, but to man's faith.

If I obey only what I understand, no faith at all is required, and *that* is the tragedy of the matter, because without faith it is impossible to please God (Hebrews 11:6). In the things of God, faith always precedes understanding, *fides quaerens intellectum*. The man that obeys because he understands is following his own lights. He is not walking in faith, and faith is the only path to understanding.

This is the reason the teaching of Sirach on this point is so offensive to modern man, who is resolved to follow his own mind, to walk by naked reason or even some lesser light. Man will never arrive at the understanding of the Law if he refuses to obey the Law, because understanding comes from obedience.

The long closing section of this chapter (vv. 15–28) may not seem, at first, to touch the moral life. In other words, these maxims do not directly deal with the difference between right and wrong. Their subject matter pertains, rather, to what we may call the "decorous," the difference between the seemly and the unseemly, the distinction between the proper and the improper, the polite and the impolite.

This is important, nonetheless. For the author of this book, the pursuit of wisdom embraces not only the morally sound but also the morally fitting. The wise man, according to these verses, is known by the way he expresses himself, even by the modulations of his humor. His moral character can be discerned in a certain delicacy of expression, the avoidance of coarseness, a measured diffidence of approach. True morality has an aesthetic aspect.

It is clear, then, what Sirach would say about Rousseau's theory of the "noble savage." He would think it nothing more than a myth. For Sirach the wise man is necessarily a *civilized* man—a citizen whose self-restraint justifies the confidence and respect of his fellow citizens.

Such a man is deeply suspicious of spontaneity, and he ascribes no great value to the ability to shock. Indeed, he will regard the impulse to shock people as a sure indication of immaturity and self-centeredness.

Against this spirit, Sirach exhorts his readers to the pursuit of *paideia*—proper instruction—and a chief characteristic of *paideia* is self-restraint. It imposes restrictions on speech and behavior. This is why the fool hates discipline. It "cramps his style." It places a fetter on his feet, a manacle on his right hand (v. 19).

Consequently, the fool is invariably on the side of spontaneity and free expression. He believes in "doing what comes naturally," because he is unable to see that what he calls "natural" pertains, in fact, to our fallen nature. Thus, the fool despises the social restraints put on human expectations by the accumulated discipline of thousands of years.

Because of this quality, the fool is easy to find. In art, literature, and music, for example, we recognize him in his pathological need to give offense. He is the so-called educator who has no respect for either tradition or discipline. He prides himself on "marching to a different drummer." Consequently there is often a lot of syncopation going on in his poor head.

For Sirach, this is not the path to wisdom, but the road to self-destruction and the downfall of the cultured life.

❧ SIRACH 22 ❧

The great enemies of wisdom are laziness and self-indulgence. Hence, Sirach stands with Proverbs in the Bible's tradition of hard work, discipline, and steady application.

In the first section of this chapter (vv. 1–18), our author gathers a collection of maxims on the subject of laziness. For him, sloth is the most obvious mark of the fool.

The fool is a problem, not only for himself, but also for others, because laziness has social consequences. Nobody wants to be around a lazy person, for the very simple reason that one person's laziness increases someone else's labor.

In this section Sirach also speaks of the young female. If she is lazy, he says, nobody will want to marry her, so she will spend her life depending on her parents (vv. 3–4). On the other hand, a shameless daughter, if she is married, brings dishonor on both her father and her husband (v. 3).

Sirach takes up the theme of corporal punishment (v. 6), which is a traditional subject in Wisdom literature (cf. Proverbs 13:24; 19:18; 22:15; 23:13–14). Even today one hears Christians debate about the wisdom of spanking naughty children, as though Holy Scripture had not settled the question.

Toward the end of this section (vv. 16–18), Sirach contrasts the stability of the wise with the instability of the fool. In both cases, we note, his concern is social, not individual.

The second section of this book is, once again, friendship. Sirach seems never to tire of speaking of friendship. It is clear that this subject is very close to his heart.

In the course of commenting on this book we have often reflected that the pursuit of wisdom is a social quest. A man attains wisdom through socialization, not in a private ahistorical sphere isolated from the normal concerns of men. The eremitic vocation does not fall within the purview of Sirach.

This is the reason Sirach places a high value on friendship (vv. 19–27). Constancy of virtuous habit, about which he spoke in the first section of this chapter, includes constancy in friendship. It is of the very nature of friendship that people grow to depend on one another.

For this reason the inconstant person makes the very worst of friends. Such a one cannot be depended on. He is not steady in his loyalties, so those who would be his friends will be disappointed. No one will be disposed to remain the friend of someone who throws a temper tantrum, for example (v. 20).

This does not mean, however, that there is no room for temper between friends (v. 21), and most friendships do have their ups and downs. What is absolutely required, however, is a sustained pattern of loyalty.

In the case of a deliberate, unprovoked attack, the damage to a friendship is often irreparable. This will especially be the case if there is an intentional, calculated violation of trust. The disclosure of personal secrets, for instance, usually means the end of a friendship (v. 22).

Our friends are especially recognized in our times of poverty and seasons of affliction (v. 22; cf. 6:8; 12:21). Loyalty during such times is sure of its reward. A true friend is also recognized as one's defender in the hour of attack (v. 25).

~: SIRACH 23 :~

Before he begins his praise of wisdom in chapter 24, Sirach intends to investigate two areas of life in which man experiences some of the strongest resistance to the fear of God—namely, speech (vv. 7–15) and sex (vv. 16–27). These are the subjects of the present chapter.

Prior to his investigation of these two subjects, however, Sirach feels the need to pray for enlightenment (vv. 1–6). He calls upon the Lord, the "Father and Master" of his life (v. 1). He prays for safekeeping from the temptations attendant on these two subjects. He asks for scourges (*mastigoi*) over his thoughts and discipline (*paideia*) over his heart. This prayer recognizes that man is unable, on his own, to avoid sin.

It is significant that this prayer is twice addressed to God as "Father," a title rarely applied to God in the Old Testament, although rather common in Jewish liturgical texts of the time. The significance of this title here in Sirach's prayer has to do with the context of scourgings and discipline.

This prayer is inspired by Proverbs 3:11–12 (LXX): "My son, do not despise the instruction (*paideias*) of the Lord, / Neither grow weary under His reproof. / For whom the Lord loves He instructs (*paidevei*); / And chastises (*mastogoi*) every son He receives."

The parallels between these two texts are obvious, as indicated in the words "scourge" (*mastichs*) and "chastening" (*paideia*) in both passages. Indeed, the reference to the scourged and disciplined "son" suggests that God is pictured as a Father.

In fact, the Hebrew text of Proverbs 3:12 reads, "For whom the Lord loves He corrects, / Just as a father the son *in whom* he delights" (*k'av 'eth ben yirtseh*).

Clearly this context of needed discipline for the young is the setting in which the Old Testament feels comfortable speaking of God as "Father." This usage is clearly metaphorical. God is a "Father" in the sense that His discipline of His children is a sign of His delight in them.

This imagery is carried over into the Epistle to the Hebrews, which offers a short commentary on these two verses of Proverbs. The author writes, "'My son, do not despise the chastening (*paideias*) of the LORD, / Nor be discouraged when you are rebuked by Him; / For whom the LORD loves He chastens (*paidevei*), / And scourges (*mastigoi*) every son whom He receives.'"

Hebrews goes on to comment on these verses: "If you endure chastening (*paideian*), God deals with you as with sons; for what son is there whom a father does not chasten (*paidevei*)? But if you are without chastening (*paideias*), of which all have become partakers, then you are illegitimate and not sons. Furthermore, we have had human fathers who corrected (*paideutas*) us, and we paid *them* respect. Shall we not much more readily be in subjection to the Father of spirits and live? For they indeed for a few days chastened (*epaidevon*) *us* as seemed *best* to them, but He for *our* profit, that *we* may be partakers of His holiness. Now no chastening (*paideia*) seems to be joyful for the present, but painful; nevertheless, afterward it yields the peaceable fruit of righteousness to those who have been trained by it" (Hebrews 12:7–11).

The noun *paideia* appears only seven times in the New Testament; four of these are in the present text in Hebrews. Noun and verb together, the root *paidev*— is found seven times in this passage.

In this commentary on the text from Proverbs, the Epistle to the Hebrews explicitly calls God a "father," by reason of the discipline He shows to His sons. This is how they recognize that they *are* sons.

Here in Sirach, however, it is more than merely accepting the discipline that comes from a loving father. Sirach actually *asks* for this discipline. He pleads for the scourging of his thoughts, the chastening of his heart. With respect to these two subjects of speech and sex, he beseeches God not to spare him those things that will safeguard his mind.

Having prayed for this discipline, Sirach then undertakes a discussion of speech (vv. 7–15) and sex (vv. 16–27).

Among the many aspects of speech worthy of consideration, Sirach is chiefly concerned here with the proper control of it. Experience tells us with respect to the tongue that some form of "service" is always involved. That is to say, man either makes his tongue serve him, or he will soon find himself in service to his tongue. If he does not take charge of his tongue, it will not be long before his tongue has assumed charge of *him*.

Left to itself, the tongue is chaotic and leads man on the path to destruction. Thus, Sirach mentions "a way of speaking comparable to death" (v. 12). What is needed, he says, is—literally—a "discipline of the mouth" (*paideian stomatos*, v. 7; "teaching of my mouth," OSB).

In this respect Sirach's chief point of caution is swearing, the taking of oaths, which is the most solemn form of speech. Indeed, most people recognize that if an oath is not taken with due solemnity, it is invariably a sin of speech, because the man that takes an oath invokes God, a thing never to be done lightly. Moreover, to take an oath at any time is to invite the judgment of God—that is the whole business of an oath.

For this reason an oath should be taken but rarely and only in special circumstances, under special and solemn control. One must not become "a man who swears many oaths" (*aner polyorkos*, v. 11).

We observe that in Sirach's mind the tongue is principally to be controlled by reverence; this is the whole point of his comments about swearing. A tongue that is reverent with the name of God, he seems to suggest, will be properly guided in all other matters. In other words, the tongue's proper restraint with regard to God is the beginning of its full correct discipline. All man's speech will be governed by reverence for God.

With respect to the control of the tongue, Sirach's precautions are well compared to those of St. James, who also appreciates the need to control the tongue, so that the tongue cannot itself *gain* control! Thus, James compares the tongue to a horse's bit: If the rider has charge of that bit, he controls the horse; if the horse takes control of the bit, the horse controls the rider (James 3:3).

James also equates the tongue to the rudder on a ship. It is the pilot's control of this very small rudder that brings even the fierce winds into the service of the ship (3:4). A single flame, which James likens to the tongue (compare Acts 2:3), can do immense harm over a wide area, unless it is brought under control (James 3:5–6). So difficult is this task, says James, that if someone "does not stumble in word, he *is* a perfect man" (3:2).

In addition to speech, Sirach directs his attention to sex as a subject fraught with dangers to the quest of wisdom (vv. 16–27). He knows—and all knowledge of history testifies—that if failure to control the tongue impedes the attainment of wisdom, this danger is augmented sevenfold in the failure to control sex.

The element of peril common to both these subjects is their essentially social nature. In the first case, we recognize that nearly all of social life is based on the experience of speech. In the second case, it is obvious that sex is the essential biological foundation for marriage and the family, which is the most elementary social institution.

The abuse of speech destroys the experience of trust, on which the whole social order depends as a foundational presupposition. Trust is the basis of political and economic life.

Sex, in turn, is the absolute condition for marriage, which is the normal source of the family. Consequently sex is the context in which the experience of trust is most especially required. In short, the social fabric absolutely requires the integrity of contractual sexual unions built on trust. Such a union is called marriage. There can be no such trust, however, without the control of sex.

For this reason Sirach concentrates his criticism against adultery above all other sexual sins. Adultery is not only a sin against chastity but also a sin against justice; adultery is the violation of a social contract. Adultery is a personal insult to one's partner in marriage, but it is also an assault on the very foundations of society. No healthy society can tolerate this, which is why the Mosaic Law prescribes death as its proper punishment.

Adultery, however, is the extreme case. All sexual sins are in some measure sins against society, which is why in the Bible they are punished by society (cf. Proverbs 5:11–14; 6:32–33).

The motive of restraint in all these matters, according to Sirach, is the fear of the Lord (v. 27) and the cultivated awareness that God sees all things. Indeed, he says, the eyes of the Lord are ten thousand times brighter than the sun (v. 19). God, who reads the heart, considers even unchaste thoughts and looks to be the equivalent of adultery (Matthew 5:27–28).

EXCURSUS:
Sirach and James
The thematic similarity between Sirach and the Epistle of James, which was noted in the previous

chapter, elicits further comparison between these two works.

The Epistle of James, though constructed in the form of a letter—identifying both the sender and those addressed—closely resembles, in both form and content, a standard set of Jewish instructions on practical wisdom. As such, it invites the same exegetical interest as other literature of the same sort, such as Proverbs and Sirach.

All three of these works are collections of apothegms connected loosely to the theme of wisdom, but arranged in an order not immediately apparent or necessarily logical. In James these moral subjects include patience in trial (1:2–4; 5:7–11), a cautious attitude toward wealth (1:9–11), compassion and solicitude for the poor (2:2–8; 5:1–6), the avoidance of rash judgment (4:11–12), and a sense of the fleeting nature of life (4:13–16).

Like Proverbs (2:3–6) and Sirach (1:1), James believes that wisdom is a gift from God (1:17; 3:15) and, as such, the proper object of prayer (1:5). Solomon himself, of course, provided the model for such prayer (3 Kingdoms 3:9–12).

Unlike the epistles of St. Paul, that of James gives little explicit attention to doctrinal concerns. Its overriding concern lies, rather, in the practical moral life of those who want to please God. Like Sirach, James insists on "doing" things (1:23; 4:11). Whereas Abraham is a model of faith for Paul (Romans 4 *passim*), for James he is a model of works (2:14–26). According to James, "true religion" has to do with moral purity and social concerns, such as the care of the needy and disadvantaged (1:27), a point on which his view is identical to that of Sirach (4:10). Like Sirach (4:6; 21:5; 35:17–18), James fears God's just response to the complaints of the oppressed or neglected poor (5:4).

For both these authors, the man approved by God will undergo trial. Indeed, James says early, "the man who endures temptation" will be blessed, "for when he has been approved, he will receive the crown of life" (1:12). Job is his model in this respect (5:11). Sirach, too, stresses the inevitability of trials for the man resolved on the service of God (2:1–5). We have already considered the importance of the Job story in the Wisdom tradition inherited by Sirach.

Control of the tongue is important to Sirach and James. According to both authors, a wise man should be quick to listen but slow to give voice to his thoughts (Sirach 5:11–12; 18:19; James 1:19).

In short, James is an example of a Christian continuation of the classical Judaic transmission of wisdom. It is striking that he does not refer his moral exhortations to specifically Christian doctrines. Indeed, except for his two explicit references to Jesus (1:1; 2:1), we would be hard pressed to say how the teaching of James differs from that of Sirach. On the contrary, his moral approach to the pursuit of wisdom seems in perfect continuity with that of the Old Testament.

❧ SIRACH 24 ❧

In the formal center of this book appears what is arguably the most important chapter, and certainly the most beautiful. Likewise, halfway through this same chapter comes Sirach's description of wisdom as "the mother of fair love, fear, understanding, and holy hope" (v. 18). This verse, roughly at the center of the entire book, may be regarded as the distilled concentration of Sirach's message.

As in Proverbs 8:22–31, on which the present chapter is obviously modeled and dependent, Sirach personifies wisdom as the first and most formal component of God's creation, the inner and intelligible core of its beauty and being. Wisdom "came forth from the mouth of the Most High / And covered the earth like a mist" (v. 3). With these words Sirach evokes the remembrance of creation's beginning, when "the Spirit of God was hovering over the face of the water" and "a fountain came up from the ground and watered the whole face of the earth" (Genesis 1:2; 2:6). Through these and other references to water (vv. 25–27, 30–31), wisdom is portrayed as giving life to creation. Indeed, she continues to live on at the heart of all things, awaiting discernment by the wise.

For all this attention to the structure of creation, nonetheless, Sirach refuses to reduce wisdom to an animistic function in man's contemplation of nature. Following the ubiquitous thesis of Holy Scripture, Sirach approaches nature through the prophetic consideration of history and tradition. Hence, he insists that wisdom has truly taken up her abode—at God's behest—in the institutions of salvation history: those associated with Israel and Jerusalem. She is especially identified with the Torah (v. 23; cf. Deut. 33:4) and the temple (vv. 8–12).

There are two large sections to this chapter: wisdom's self-description (vv. 1–22) and Sirach's subsequent meditation on this subject (vv. 23–34).

Wisdom is portrayed in this chapter as a creature, not a divine being. Her personification is determined grammatically by the feminine nouns for "wisdom" in both Hebrew (*hokma*) and Greek (*sophia*), not through identification with a goddess. (*Feminine* is, after all, a category of grammar, whereas *female* is a category of being. Sirach, accordingly, conceives of wisdom as feminine, not female.) For this reason, the present writer believes there is no merit to the modern suggestion that Sirach may have been influenced by the cult of Isis or some other female divinity. This suggestion is difficult to support, being completely out of character with the theological tenor of the book.

In this chapter's description of wisdom, Sirach joins several strands of late Jewish piety: the traditional wisdom meditation (as in Proverbs 8 and the Wisdom of Solomon 6), the intelligence of the Torah, and motifs of Israel's liturgical worship. His comparison of wisdom to several trees and bushes (vv. 13–17) lays a particular stress on her beauty and vitality. This emphasis, in turn, leads to an invitation to eat of wisdom's fruits (vv. 19–22).

As Sirach began this chapter with the dawn of creation, so he ends it with the dawn of his own teaching, when he "will yet make instruction shine like the morning" (v. 32). Here he shows himself to be aware of his responsibility, as a rabbi, to leave the inherited instruction "behind for future generations" (v. 33). Sirach does not labor for himself alone, but "for all who seek wisdom" (v. 34).

∾ SIRACH 25 ∾

There are two major parts to the present chapter: a series of apothegms based largely on numbered sequences (vv. 1–11), and a description of an evil wife (vv. 12–25).

The first part is not united by theme but by construction: There are two numbered sequences (vv. 1–2 and 7–11), separated by a meditation on the wisdom of the aged (vv. 3–6). We will remark on these in order.

Sirach lists three things beautiful (v. 1) and three detestable (v. 2). All three of the first, we observe, are social: happy marriage, solid families, harmonious neighborhoods. To these are contrasted an arrogant pauper, a mendacious man of wealth, and a lecherous elder (of the sort found in the story of chaste Susannah in the Book of Daniel). This last character, the adulterous old man, is immediately contrasted with a wise elder (vv. 3–6) and, at the end of the chapter, will find his counterpart in the evil wife (vv. 14–28).

Sirach's description of "the beauty of old men"—their wisdom and grey hair—puts the present writer in mind of Alessandro Manzoni's lengthy depiction of the venerable Federico Borromeo in *I Promessi Sposi*. When the villainous Unnamed encounters the *bellezza senile* of Federico, he is held spellbound by the wise grace that emanates from the white hair, benign face, and graceful carriage of the old man. Faced with this incarnation of wisdom, the villain is miraculously converted on the spot. This is the turning point of Manzoni's great novel.

In the ten blessings enumerated in Sirach's second sequence (vv. 7–11), he again starts with the graces of the domestic life and goes on to speak of man's other social settings. These blessings are then contrasted with the burden and curse of being married to an evil woman. This final character is described, it would seem, in such a way as to provide a warning to the young man who has not yet chosen a wife. Alas, this most important decision of a person's life is sometimes made under the impulse of blind fascination, without proper preparation, discernment, or clarity of thought. The character Federico, one recalls—in both historical fact and Manzoni's fiction—was unmarried!

Sirach's depiction of the evil wife sets up his presentation of the good wife at the beginning of the next chapter.

✣ Sirach 26 ✣

The first part of this chapter (vv. 1–18) continues the last chapter's contrast between a wicked and a virtuous wife. Among the virtues a wise man hopes to find in a wife is, above all, a sense of peace and quiet (25:20). This becomes ever more necessary over the years. It is common among men that, as they grow older, they tend to talk less and to cherish a quiet atmosphere. A quiet atmosphere is more conducive to thought, and as a man grows in wisdom, he is more disposed to *think*. The last thing such a man needs is a lot of yak-yak-yak. On the contrary, he hopes to find in his wife a source of peace (v. 2). This is among the Lord's choicest blessings (v. 3).

A wicked wife, on the contrary, is worse than a riot in the streets (v. 5). Among the vices of such a woman, Sirach mentions jealousy (v. 6), physical vanity (v. 9), drunkenness, gossiping, and immodesty (v. 8).

What is said about wives goes double for daughters, concerning whom Sirach warns that they should not be given much liberty (v. 10). Don't be surprised, he says, when they disobey you. This is what they do (v. 11). Sirach is particularly explicit and graphic in his warnings about sexual license among daughters (v. 12).

Our author then returns to the theme of the quiet and discreet wife (v. 13), asserting that "a silent wife is a gift from the Lord" (v. 14). She is the sunshine of the home (v. 16) and grows more beautiful with age (v. 17). In saying these things, Sirach suggests that such reflections are the mark of a wise man.

Having considered the proper maintenance of the home, Sirach moves outside the home (vv. 19–21) to treat of livelihood, more specifically through some form of commerce. (Clearly he is thinking of an urban, not an agrarian, setting.)

In this regard Sirach recommends the same caution that was necessary within the home, because the commercial life also is fraught with many moral dangers. As the home is governed by proper discipline over sexuality, so a man's life of labor is governed by a proper vigilance with respect to greed and dishonesty.

Verses 21–27 are found in only a few manuscripts and are generally not considered part of the canonical text; thus the OSB omits them.

~: Sirach 27 :~

The author continues the theme introduced at the very end of the previous chapter, the moral integrity required in the pursuit of earning a living.

Sirach perceives a deep problem (vv. 1–8), which may be described as follows: Men of business are sensitive to a thing called opportunity. They develop a sense of how events are unfolding. If this sense is highly developed, commercial men learn how to take advantage of the future. They can become very good at this pursuit; they become wealthy. Since the purpose of commerce is the attaining of wealth, such men will necessarily set the standard in the world of commerce. There is obviously nothing wrong with this.

Suppose, however, that this sense of opportunity is accompanied by a moral insensitivity. Suppose the *opportunity* can be helped along with a slight recourse to subterfuge, a reluctance to disclose the facts, a faint shading in one's moral judgment in the direction of one's own economic advantage. Sirach weighs the gravity of temptations to dishonesty and subterfuge. He knows the lure of fraud and deception. He appreciates the difficulty of remaining completely sincere and perfectly honest in matters of business.

He also knows how a certain cynicism may assert itself in the realm of business, a kind of moral callousness. Many individuals, aware in their own hearts of a disposition to deceive, easily presume that other men will also succumb to this disposition. Indeed, there arises a common expectation of deception. Rather readily it is assumed that human beings cannot be trusted in monetary and commercial matters. There arises a loss of the fiduciary sense within society.

In these circumstances dishonesty tends to become, in some sense, the norm and, as the norm, acceptable. If there are no eternal moral principles to guide the man of business, he will be guided by whatever is socially correct, and it is a matter of observable fact that a dishonest society will find dishonesty socially acceptable.

Indeed, in these circumstances merchants, businessmen, and financial brokers will begin to presume that dishonesty is necessary to their success. Integrity, they imagine, will surely lead to loss and failure. When this frame of mind prevails, as it often has, social and economic pressures make honesty a difficult choice. Sirach weighs these pressures and finds them daunting.

On the other hand, honesty and integrity are necessary and essential to the quest of wisdom. Does this mean that a man of business can never become a wise man? Is it the case that an investor is forever barred from virtue, or that a merchant can in no wise be righteous? Sirach fears an incompatibility between the quest for wisdom and the pursuit of wealth (v. 2).

Although he fears such an incompatibility, he does not think it inevitable, for he goes on to say that the man who seeks for wisdom will find it and shall wear it like a robe (v. 8). It cannot be the case that there is an inevitable opposition between virtue and the life of commerce.

There are two reasons for supposing this. First, virtuous men are not really so rare in the mercantile and financial worlds. If one is sensitive to their presence, one may meet them all the time. These individuals stand as strong empirical evidence against a supposed opposition between virtue and the commercial life.

Second, such an opposition between virtue and commerce would posit a thesis of moral despair. It would effectively bar wisdom from the realm of commerce by putting the quest of wealth outside the influence of virtue. It would prevent wise men from taking part in much of social life. In doing so, it would attack the moral structure of human existence.

Sirach's reflections on this problem, therefore, are not speculative but practical and exhortatory. Knowing the difficulty of remaining honest in the acquisition of wealth, he does not presume that all men will be up to the challenge of the task.

∽ SIRACH 28 ∾

Our author begins this chapter with an exhortation to avoid revenge (vv. 1–11). Vengeance, we recall, was among man's first sins (Genesis 4:14–15, 23–24). Simply as a matter of history, this is one of the earliest sins that man *learned*; it was among his primary experiences in sin. Hence, the impulse to revenge lies near the base of man's defining memory. It is one of the chief ways in which death reigns in his flesh.

Consequently, to be reborn in grace the human soul—the *psyche* of man—must be fortified by the resolve to put away all expressions of vengeance, because they are most serious impediments to the Holy Spirit's influence on the heart.

Sirach begins by observing that those who seek revenge will receive the vengeance of God (v. 1). In fact, this warning was addressed first to Cain: "Whoever kills Cain, vengeance shall be taken on him sevenfold" (Genesis 4:15).

Not only must the wise man not seek vengeance, Sirach goes on, but also he must actively *forgive* those who hurt him. Sirach makes this obligation an imperative of prayer (v. 2), a teaching taken up by Jesus in His prayer, "And forgive us our debts, as we forgive our debtors" (Matthew 6:12). Jesus went on to comment, "For if you forgive men their trespasses, your heavenly Father will also forgive you. But if you do not forgive men their trespasses, neither will your Father forgive your trespasses" (6:14–15).

If we seek the forgiveness of God, says Sirach, we do well not to withhold such forgiveness from our neighbor. On this theme Jesus gave the parable of the unforgiving servant (Matt. 18:23–35).

In Sirach's teaching on this subject, we are well beyond the *lex talionis* that Jesus declared to be abrogated: "You have heard that it was said, 'An eye for an eye and a tooth for a tooth.' But I tell you not to resist an evil person. But whoever slaps you on your right cheek, turn the other to him also" (Matt. 5:38–39).

Sirach, who anticipates the Gospel in this matter, represents a great moral advance, which is expressed in three rhetorical questions (vv. 3–5).

The correct perspective on this subject, says Sirach, is given by the remembrance of death and the judgment of God (vv. 6–7). This is the thought, moreover, best designed to put away all wrath and wrangling (vv. 8–11).

In the latter part of this chapter (vv. 12–26), Sirach has recourse to colorful imagery to describe the moral ironies of the tongue. In this respect he will put the attentive reader very much in mind of the Epistle of James (3:2–12). His first metaphor is that of a spark (v. 12; cf. James 3:5–6), still small enough to be either encouraged or extinguished by what comes out of the mouth. Which is to say, the mouth controls the situation, so the man who controls his tongue controls everything. Indeed, this is a favorite topic of the Book of Sirach (5:12—6:1; 19:5–16; 20:17–25; 23:7–15).

It is clear that Sirach's preoccupation with the tongue is directed mainly at the social life of human beings, and for this reason he speaks on this subject immediately after his treatment of anger (vv. 7–11). Hence, he first warns against the spreading of rumors, especially by the "double-tongued man" (*diglosson*, v. 13; "deceitful," OSB).

This last metaphor suggests the malicious person who publishes rumors back and forth in two directions, inciting enmity on both sides. Such activity is especially malicious and demonic. Whole nations have perished because of such people, because their sins lead to war (v. 14).

The "slanderous" or "meddlesome" tongue in this verse is literally a "third tongue" (*glossa trité*), a striking metaphor indicating a vile person whose speech becomes the mediating instrument of mutual hatred and animosity. In rabbinical literature this expression designates the slanderer.

Is it significant that the author immediately mentions women whose reputations have been destroyed by this vice (v. 15)?

From his social concern with the tongue, Sirach turns to a psychological consideration, observing that exposure to contentious speech destroys peace of soul (v. 16). The tongue, he says, can inflict wounds more serious than the whip or the sword (vv. 17–18). Only a very inexperienced person will say, "Words can never hurt me." It is a simple fact of observation that words can absolutely destroy us.

Indeed, the tongue becomes the instrument of bondage in those that abuse it (vv. 19–20). It is more deadly than the grave (v. 21).

Some of us are old enough to remember the American writer Truman Capote, whose final years were embittered by his lifelong penchant for rumor-mongering. After years of great popularity among the elite trendsetters in American culture, he came to a very sad death almost without friends, nearly all of whom abandoned him in his closing years because he had betrayed them with his rumors.

Only the fear of God can deliver a man from the bondage of the tongue (vv. 22, 24–26). A man either controls his tongue or is controlled by his tongue. Sirach ends by returning to his original metaphor, the flame or spark (v. 23), which, as we have seen, is a favorite of St. James.

❧ SIRACH 29 ❧

From the subject of speech Sirach moves to a consideration of money, another and important aspect of man's social nature, and the mutual trust that makes social life possible (vv. 1–20). If Sirach is cautious about the use of speech, he is even more so about the use of money. Both are instruments of social life that easily elude responsible control.

Sirach starts his treatment of this subject by urging the mercy that will move a man to lend to his neighbor in time of need (v. 1). We observe here that mercy is the motive for lending. In our own culture, where lending money is a means of *making* money, this is an aspect of lending that is readily lost. Holy Scripture, however, looks rather askance at lending money at interest, considering the practice only a form of exploiting someone's misfortune. A capitalist system of economics, in which invested money is used to stimulate and sustain financial growth, is simply unknown in the Bible. Its moral justification cannot be established simply by quoting biblical texts.

When Holy Scripture considers the lending of money, the consideration runs along very simple moral lines: Money is either lent without interest as an act of mercy, or it is lent with interest as an exploitation of someone's poverty. The Bible recommends the former and condemns the latter.

Even in showing mercy by lending, however, there are practical perils to be avoided. Specifically, the person who lends his money runs the risk of losing it (v. 6). Loans are to be repaid; this is not an act of charity but a dictate of justice. That is to say, borrowed money still belongs to the one who lent it.

There must be no duplicity about this (v. 4). A loan should not be treated as a windfall of some sort, prompting the borrower to become deceitful, dilatory, or dishonest with the lender (v. 5). Such behavior disheartens men from making loans in the future (v. 7). The dilatory borrower hurts those in need at some further time by discouraging the promptings of mercy in someone otherwise disposed to lend.

On the other hand, if a man repays a loan, it is reasonable that he should be able to borrow again in the future (v. 3).

Even if a loan is not repaid, nonetheless, the lender should not become despondent. He should consider a bad loan as a form of alms and not lose the generous spirit that prompted him to lend the money in the first place (vv. 8–9). Better it is to lose the money for the sake of charity than to keep it for the sake of selfishness (v. 10).

We lay up treasure, says Sirach, when we deposit our money with the poor (vv. 11–12), because money given in alms will return to deliver us in our affliction (vv. 13–14). He also exhorts the one who has received alms not to be unfaithful to the man who helped him (v. 15). To act otherwise is sinful and ungrateful (vv. 16–19).

Nonetheless, Sirach, even as he recommends it, shares the ancient caution about going surety for someone. Great houses have been thus brought to ruin, he recalls, when someone imprudently cosigned on a loan (vv. 18–19; cf. Proverbs 11:15; 17:18; 22:26).

These exhortations to charity with our financial resources are logically followed by corresponding instructions favoring frugality and simplicity of life (vv. 21–28). The person who lives on bread and water, he reminds us, at least enjoys the advantage of being financially independent. After all, he asks, what good is a lavish lifestyle if all one's possessions really belong to someone else? One should not go into debt for frivolous reasons, and a strong personal discipline and prudence are necessary in these matters.

❧ SIRACH 30 ☙

Their subject matters divide this chapter into two halves. The first half, verses 1–13, is concerned with the proper raising of children; the second, verses 14–25, deals with matters of personal health.

The first half (vv. 1–13) directs the reader's attention to the practical matter of how to raise children, a subject on which our author has already commented several times. Indeed, the topic of childrearing provides the underlying context and preoccupation of this whole book, as it does for all the more ancient Wisdom literature—the Book of Proverbs, for example. The wisdom sought in the Books of Proverbs and Sirach is the more traditional form, emphasizing the transmission of practical wisdom from one generation to the next. The accent in this literature falls on moral inheritance. It is preeminently educational in nature, neither exploratory nor speculative. It is directed to the uncomplicated raising of the young.

The present book, and more specifically these verses, recognizes that what is learned early in life gives form to a person's character. While it is always possible for a man to transcend the limits of his early education, it seems that few people actually succeed in doing so. We see evidence that this fact is generally recognized in the custom of referring to a man's formative education even when he has grown very old. Thus, when an eighty-year-old guest lecturer is introduced, it is often the case that reference is made to the schools from which he graduated many decades earlier, even though the lecturer in question knows vastly more than he did when he graduated. (In such circumstances a reference like this can be downright embarrassing when the person in question remembers himself as pretty deficient on the day of his graduation!) Still, such references represent a persuasion about the importance of early education.

Sirach too recognizes this importance, a fact that explains why he recommends the maintenance of discipline over the growing child and even physical expressions of such discipline (vv. 1–2).

Special attention is deserved by the participial subjects that begin each of the first three verses of this chapter: "The man who loves his son" (*ho agapon ton huion avtou*, v. 1), "he who disciplines his son" (*ho paidevon to huion avtou*, v. 2), and "the man who teaches his son" (*ho didaskon ton huion avtou*). This triple parallel construction is a sort of hendiatris, suggesting that all three participles refer to the same thing designated in three ways: loving, disciplining, and teaching. Put into noun form, this triple parallel may indicate that Sirach sees no substantial difference between love, discipline, and education.

It may also be the case that Sirach intends to indicate a progression—love providing discipline, discipline leading to education.

When a good parent dies, he does so in the confidence that he has left a good person on the earth, an enemy of evil (vv. 4–6). A pandering parent, on the other hand, someone who spoils and overindulges the child, really cannot die soon enough, because he will start paying for his failure almost immediately (vv. 7–13). One recalls the failure of Eli as a parent in the early chapters of 1 Samuel.

The second half of this chapter (vv. 14–25) is about good health. In the Sermon on the Mount Jesus asks the rhetorical question, "Is not life more than food and the body more than clothing?" (Matthew 6:25). Neither great insight nor advanced wisdom is required to grasp the truth contained in this question. It is a matter perfectly obvious to a second's reflection. This is the reason our Lord poses the truth in a rhetorical question.

Any intelligent person knows that the body is more important than the clothing that adorns it. Everyone knows this, yet there are men who destroy their health by overworking in order to obtain more wealth. This is folly. Just as health is superior to wealth, so poverty is preferable to sickness (vv. 14–16).

This priority explains the sequence of Sirach's structure at this point. Our author reflects on the importance of health before he goes on to consider the subject of wealth in the following chapter (31:1–11).

In these verses about good health, a first feature to be noticed is Sirach's indifference to any great separation between physical and psychic health. A true Hebrew in this respect, he is not interested in opposing the body to the soul, or vice versa, because both are composites of a single entity. A sick soul is not good for the body, nor a sick body good for the soul.

St. Francis of Sales remarked someplace that few people grow holier during times of illness. It can happen, of course, but the phenomenon is rare and not normally to be expected.

The reason for this is simple. The soul reacts to the dispositions and impulses of the body. If the body is languid and torpid, the mind tends to become dull and the will weak. Dull thinking, however, and a flaccid will are not conducive to growth in holiness.

At the same time, nonetheless, a melancholy spiritual state brings its own pressures to bear on the body. Depression of mind and emotions can be very destructive of physical well-being. And what is true of depressing thoughts is also true of anger and envy. Both are destructive to the body as well as the soul (v. 24).

We recall the example of Nabal in 1 Kingdoms 25. He was a driven man of surly disposition, whose servants described him to Abigail, his wife, "For he is such a son of mischief that no one can speak to him" (25:17). A few verses later Abigail describes Nabal to David, "Please, let not my lord set his heart against this man of pestilence. For as his name is, so is he. His name is Nabal, and folly is with him" (25:25).

Alas, we also recall what happened to Nabal: This unhealthy state of mind and disposition eventually brought him to an early grave. Holy Scripture relates of him, "his heart died within him, and he became like a stone. And it came to pass about ten days later that the Lord struck Nabal and he died" (25:38). Even though his symptoms seem to suggest a stroke, it is instructive to observe that the Bible says Nabal died of heart failure. This is not a heart attack in the strict sense, I think, but something more spiritual. His heart became like a stone. One meets such hearts from time to time. In the case of Nabal, the spiritual problem eventually became a physical problem, and Nabal was no match for the challenge.

A happy disposition, on the other hand, serves the cause of physical health. A prudent man, consequently, will avoid those things that make a happy disposition more difficult (v. 21). A wise man will deliberately cultivate joy, if only for the sake of his health (v. 22). He does what he can to avoid compulsive morbid thoughts. He *fights* depression and regards it as his foe. Indeed, depression is not safely entertained; it is an enemy that must be given no quarter, no caucus, no compromise. It must be beaten away without mercy, like taking a heavy club to a rabid dog.

~: SIRACH 31 :~

Two subjects are treated in this chapter: wealth (vv. 1–11) and table etiquette (31:12—32:12).

Having instructed his readers about health (30:14–25), Sirach now directs their attention to the subject of wealth (vv. 1–11). The link between these themes is the danger of destroying one's health by an excessive effort in the accumulation of riches. Money, that is to say, often becomes the object of inordinate desire, which causes a person to forget that both his soul and his body are more important. In cases such as this, there are serious physical and moral dangers attendant on the pursuit of riches.

First, says Sirach, is the loss of sleep, which he ascribes to anxiety about money (vv. 1–2). He describes this symptom as a point of pathology. Next comes overeating, a fault rendered easier by wealth (v. 3).

Next he moves to moral dangers, the first being greed (vv. 5–6). From greed the afflicted man passes on to idolatry, making wealth an idol, to which he is disposed to sacrifice everything else (v. 7).

History provides numerous examples of this phenomenon. From ancient mythology we recall the "Midas touch," named for the Phrygian king ruined by greed. His famous story was preserved by Ovid and somewhat adjusted by Nathaniel Hawthorne in *Twice-Told Tales*. The prophet Habakkuk (1:16) wrote of those fishermen that "sacrifice unto their net." From a time closer to our own we think of Ayn Rand, who had a large dollar sign erected in the floral arrangements beside her casket. These are all rather obvious examples of financial idolatry.

Indeed, it is curious how much a bank can resemble a church: The atmosphere is hushed, quiet like a place of worship. One would almost think the tellers, gazing out at the congregation from the frames along their iconostas, were saints waiting to receive the offerings of the faithful and to distribute rich blessings hidden from view in the deeper recesses of the sanctuary. Perhaps this is why bank robbery is so heinous a crime, having about it a sacrilegious quality, as it were, something like the violation of a shrine. I think it would be very easy to worship in a bank, provided one had the appropriate sort of god.

Because the pursuit of wealth is fraught with so many moral dangers, Sirach exhibits a special respect for the rich man who has not succumbed to them (vv. 8–10). Such a man will be recognized by his generosity in the giving of alms (v. 11).

The second part of chapter 31 (vv. 12–31) is taken up with table etiquette, a subject that will extend into the next chapter.

Contemporary man does not normally think of table manners as part of the quest of wisdom, I suspect, but in the Book of Sirach the connection is taken for granted.

After all, if wisdom is a social pursuit and not an individual endeavor (a point that we have found repeatedly in the mind of Sirach), it is not difficult to discern why table etiquette pertains to the quest of wisdom. It is at table that human beings are domesticated, so to speak. It is during meals that children increase, not only "in stature," but also "in wisdom" (Luke 2:52). They learn to exercise certain patterns of personal restraint that prepare them for life in the larger society.

In learning this restraint, which pertains to language and posture as well as eating, young human beings are instructed in the joys and fellowship of what is called "conviviality"—literally "living in common." Indeed, it is arguable that the lessons learned at the family table are more fundamental to the pursuit of wisdom than are the lessons learned in the classroom. It is at meals that souls are nourished, as well as bodies. It is largely at the family table that the human character is formed.

"Character," a Greek word, means "internal shape." It is an imposed shape. Generally, a forest does not have character; a plowed field does. Indeed, "character" is related to the Greek verb *charasso*, which means "to plow." A character is imposed on a subject, like the lines made by a plow or the etchings on a coin.

The forming of a character necessarily involves restraint, perhaps even repression, because at table certain restraints are to be rigorously enforced. Certain things may not be said or done at table, and certain other things *must* be said or done at table. Otherwise there is no chance of conviviality. The eater must conform to a standard, which is to say, he must adopt as his own a "form" common to those who share the blessings of the table.

First, a child learns to pray at table, to thank God for His blessings, some of which the family shares at mealtime. He thus acquires the habit of gratitude, which is essential to a soul pleasing to God. A person who does not pray at meals acts no better than a dog or a pig.

Second, because he has just thanked God for the food given to him, the child is not permitted to complain about the food. This would be a contradiction of the prayer of thanksgiving he has just said. On the contrary, the child eats what is put in front of him, without complaint. He is properly given no choice or say in the matter. In this way he learns to accept what life offers him and does not entertain the fancy that life must conform to his own preferences. This lesson is essential to the formation of his character.

Third, the child learns to use restraint in the act of eating. He is not permitted to gorge himself like a mule. He thus acquires the habit of controlling his passions, a lesson essential to the formation of his character.

Fourth, at the family table the child learns the formalities of speech common to a polite society. He acquires the ability to communicate with others politely, a trait also indispensable to the contouring of his character.

Such disciplines at table are necessary to the correct socializing of the child. He learns to think of himself as—and feel himself to be—part of the larger social reality, gradually gaining an awareness of his place and duties in that society.

The man who learns these lessons early will someday be known for the graciousness and generosity of his table, which will endear him to many (v. 23).

What restraints are necessary with respect to food, cautions Sirach, must be doubled with regard to wine (vv. 25–31).

❧ SIRACH 32 ❧

This chapter is divided into two parts, the first (vv. 1–13) continuing the theme of table etiquette from the previous chapter, and the second comprising a series of prudential maxims loosely connected (vv. 14–24).

Whereas the foregoing chapter was chiefly concerned with the behavior of those invited to the table, the present one begins with the host at the table (vv. 1–3). This person must be gracious, first of all, and put himself at the service of the guests. To quote from another Source on this subject, the host is not at the table in order to be served, but to serve. He is the one responsible, for instance, for the quality of the wine (John 2:8–10).

The host at the table is also the one responsible for setting the tone of the conversation, especially to see that it does not become too serious. Heavy subjects of conversation are not usually compatible with conviviality, the quality that should prevail during times of meals. A pleasant conversation is the crown of the well-ordered meal.

Certain subjects of conversation should be postponed until a more propitious time; meals are not a proper setting for a display of erudition (v. 4). While it is true that man does not live by bread alone, meals are the occasions when bread should get the bulk of the attention.

Sirach especially recommends music and wine at meals (vv. 4–6). That is to say, meals should be hearty and enjoyable. They are not the proper forum for deep thoughts that are hard to follow. It is especially important to avoid controversial subjects during a meal, because these render the experience less pleasant.

Above all, one must avoid theological disputation during a meal. In this respect Tertullian observes, "a controversy about the Scriptures can effect nothing, it is clear, except to trouble a man's stomach or his brain" (*nihil proficiat congressio Scripturarum nisi plane ut aut stomachi quis ineat eversionem aut cerebri*—De Praescriptione 16). Given what we know of Tertullian, he was likely speaking from experience!

From earliest times Christians have always been forbidden to eat with heretics. Perhaps one of the sentiments supporting that prohibition was a desire to make sure that meals were times of entirely enjoyable conversations.

The proper place of young people at meals is that of learners. Consequently, it is expected that they will mainly listen and not speak. Indeed, Sirach prescribes that they remain silent and not express their views until they have been asked at least twice to do so (v. 7).

All views expressed at table, our author continues, should be given in a few words that have been carefully thought through. The ideal is a certain economy of expression whereby a substantial sum is related in few words (v. 8).

Special respect to "age" is proper at table (v. 9), a principle that applies to both men and wine. Older people have already heard it all many times. The old do not need to hear, once again—nor should they be expected to listen to—the opinions of the young and inexperienced.

Sirach goes on to make a point that is also applicable in places other than at table. Namely, a man should be extremely careful in receiving praise and not be too prompt to use that praise as capital for further conversation. Often enough that praise will be followed quickly by some ill-considered remark that brings confusion to the speaker. Embarrassment follows praise rather as thunder follows lightning (v. 10; cf. Matthew 16:17–23). Few times are more dangerous for a man than when he is being praised.

One should not linger too long after the meal, says Sirach, but hurry home (v. 12) and thank God for the pleasant evening (v. 13).

In the second half of this chapter (vv. 14–24), a rather loosely joined set of helpful proverbs, verses 14–15 form a synonymous parallel. This means that the essential message in each, especially in their first halves, is identical to the other. Specifically, what verse 14 calls the fear of the Lord is identical to what verse 15 calls the quest of the Law. These considerations are inseparable in the mind of Sirach.

Verse 15 also speaks of the "hypocrite," a term that in context refers to a person who knows the Law but is deliberately neglecting it. Such seems to be the sense of the participial form used here, *hypokrinomenos*, "hypocritizing" or "dissembling" (also in 33:2).

This category of hypocrite will become an important motif later on in the Gospels and in the relations between the early Christians and the rabbinical Judaism of New Testament times. Indeed, in the *Didache*, a Christian work of the late first century, the very name "hypocrites" has become a synonym for "Jews."

In the context of Sirach's own time, however, the word refers to those sophisticated Jews who were completely familiar with the Torah but neglected its observance as being out of step with the prevalent Greek culture and philosophy. People of this sort wanted to remain Jews but still be in favor among Gentiles. They were reluctant to be thought backward by those currently in favor. Such a person, wrote Sirach, was "offended," literally "scandalized" (*skandalisthesetai*), by the Torah. He was ashamed of his religion.

Using this same category, the apostle Paul will speak of the cross of Jesus as a *skandalon* to the Jews (1 Corinthians 1:23).

Sirach, pursuing this thought in the following verse (16), speaks of justice as a light, indicating a chief benefit of instruction from the Torah. Once again, this benefit of justice is contrasted with the intentionally cultivated relativism of the sinner, whose imagination looks for excuses to do anything his perverse will desires.

Our author next writes of the importance of seeking counsel, probably a consideration prompted by the evil willfulness of the sinner (vv. 18–19; cf. 33:29). The man who has sought and found appropriate counsel should then proceed without second thoughts and irrational fears.

Although a wise man will avoid an obviously rocky path (v. 20), he will also be wary on a path that seems to be without obstacles (v. 21).

❧ SIRACH 33 ☙

In the Bible, as in the Perennial Philosophy, the quest of wisdom makes certain presuppositions with respect to reality, or being. The chief of these presuppositions has to do with the very question of *structure*. After all, there are many schools of thought that deny that reality *is* structured; they question the very concept of an intelligent design in reality, in its stead postulating that all being is radically chaotic and amorphous, having neither design nor purpose.

Against philosophies of this sort, the Bible and the Perennial Philosophy start the quest for wisdom by presupposing that there really *is* a wisdom waiting to be found. In the Perennial Philosophy, represented by such figures as Aristotle, Plato, and the ancient thinkers of Hinduism, this wisdom gives intelligible structure to the world, the existence in which man finds himself. The world can be understood, because it is put together with understanding.

The Bible goes beyond this. In the Bible the divine wisdom gives structure and meaning, not only to the created world, but also to the human history that unfolds within that world. That is to say, in the Bible there is divine significance, not only to what God does, but also to what man does. It is the conviction of Holy Scripture that the Lord intrudes His merciful influence into human history in order to redeem, elevate, and transform the race of men. This is why Christians believe in God as the Lord of history.

Although human history appears to be all chaos, it is the teaching of the Bible that the grace of God gives form, direction, and purpose to that supposed chaos in order to bring about what is called the Kingdom of God. One finds this theme in the prophets and the Psalms, and preeminently in Jesus and the writers of the New Testament.

In the Bible's Wisdom literature this theme is especially developed in the Book of Sirach, in which the culminating chapters are devoted to the wisdom of God revealed in Israel's history. This is the study of what theology calls the doctrine of divine Providence.

The first part of the present chapter (vv. 1–18) gently introduces this theme. The author begins with an exhortation to trust in God's provision, which will preserve His servants in times of trial and temptation (v. 1). This preservation is contrasted with the lot of the hypocrite (*hypokrinomenos*, as in 32:15), whose experience of life is like a ship tossed on the wild seas (v. 2). That is to say, the structured order and meaning contained in the Torah and the prophetic oracles preserve the Lord's servant from utter chaos (v. 3).

There are other images descriptive of the hypocrite and fool. His head resembles the wheel of a cart, going round and round (v. 5). He is like a wild stallion, difficult to control (v. 6).

The Lord, in His dealings with human history, recognizes certain distinctions among men, although all men are descended from Adam (v. 10). These distinctions are hardly surprising, because the same Lord makes distinctions among days, even though all days are illumined by the same sun (vv. 7–9). Not only does God make the peoples different from one another (v. 11), says Sirach, but also He assigns to each a different task. Indeed, there is a hierarchy in man's history, as there is in man's worship (v. 12).

Taking up an image developed in Jeremiah 18:2–6 (cf. Isaiah 64:8), Sirach sees the Lord as the Potter, the Craftsman in ceramics, who gives shape to various kinds of pots, each with a different purpose (v. 13; Romans 9:21–24). This image is not a denial of man's free will, on which Sirach has already insisted (15:11–20). It asserts, rather, that men's own choices in history are made to serve God's purposes. Although good and evil men are distinguished by their own decisions, that distinction becomes a creative instrument in God's guiding hand (vv. 14–15). Both good and evil, each in its own way, work to bring about God's intentions in history. This passage later inspires Paul's theology of the dialectics of biblical history (Romans 8—11).

From the theology of history in the first part of this chapter (vv. 1–18), Sirach descends to the consideration of such mundane subjects as households and servants (vv. 19–33).

Writing for heads of households, our author warns against weakening the authority (*exsousia*) inherent in that responsibility. He manifests a strong sense of headship, on which the safety, prosperity, and stability of the household depend. This *exsousia* must not be relinquished, he says, to a wife, a son, a brother, or a friend (v. 19). That is to say, a husband and father in a home must not permit himself to become something else, because he owes this responsibility to the rest of the household (v. 21). Someone who has his father for his friend, has neither.

This unabashedly patriarchal attitude, while entirely consistent with biblical teaching as a whole, presents something of an affront to modern sensibilities, which prefer a more egalitarian, democratic, and even androgynous approach to the maintenance of a home. On the other hand, this more modern approach is arguably related to the greater instability characteristic of many modern families.

At the same time, Sirach reflects, the head of a household bears also the corresponding duty to live a blameless and honorable life (v. 22). He should personally deserve the respect elicited by his position of headship.

Sirach's subsequent comments on slavery should be regarded as a recognition that society itself is naturally hierarchical, not egalitarian (vv. 24–28). Moreover, his exhortations to treat a slave like a brother or a friend demonstrate the respectful attitude of one who recognizes that all human beings are made in God's image and likeness (vv. 29–31).

EXCURSUS:
A Modern Parable

What should be the response of today's world to Sirach's tolerance of slavery? No self-respecting modern Westerner will say that he favors slavery. Yet, a strong case can be made that the international slave trade is currently larger than it has ever been. Socially "enlightened" people, however, are blissfully unaware of this. Today's international slave trade travels rather far under the radar systems of the contemporary media.

Those in government, however, know better. Indeed, there is a special office within the United States Department of State that closely monitors the contemporary international slave trade. It is found, not only in the Third World, but in the more "enlightened" industrialized nations of the West, including the United States (for example, df. http://www.afajournalal.org/2004/april/404culture.asp). "Enlightened" people can be very naïve on a subject like this. Perhaps we can make the point by considering two contrasting attitudes towards serfdom illustrated in Leo Tolstoy's *Anna Karenina*.

On the one hand, the city dweller and philosopher, Sergei Ivanovich Koznishev, rhapsodizes about the "people," meaning the peasants who worked in the fields: "Sergei Ivanovich used to say that he knew and liked 'the people,' and he often talked to the peasants, which he knew how to do without affectation or condescension, and from every such conversation he would deduce general conclusions in favor of 'the people' and in confirmation of his knowing them." It was all talk, however. It never crossed the mind of Sergei Ivanovich to go out into the fields and work with the "people."

His brother, Konstantin Levin, on the other hand, held no such high view of the "people." He did not believe that all men are equal. On the contrary, to Levin "'the people' was simply the chief partner in the common labor." He did not idealize the peasants; indeed, he knew them to be sometimes guilty of "carelessness, slovenliness, drunkenness and lying."

Tolstoy goes on, "If he had been asked whether he liked or didn't like 'the people,' Konstantin Levin would have been absolutely at a loss what to reply. He liked and did not like 'the people,' just as he liked and did not like men in general. Of course, being a goodhearted man, he liked men more than he disliked them, and so too with 'the people.' But like or dislike 'the people' as something peculiar he could not, not only because he lived with 'the people,' and all his interests were bound up with theirs, but also because he regarded himself as a part of 'the people,' did not see any peculiar qualities or failings distinguishing himself from 'the people,' and could not contrast himself with them. Moreover, although he had lived so long in the closest relations with the peasants, as farmer and arbitrator, and what was more, as adviser . . . ., he had no definite views of 'the people,' and would have been as much at a loss to answer the question whether he knew 'the people' as the question whether he liked them. For him to say he knew 'the people' would have been the same as to say he knew men. He was continually watching and getting to know people of all sorts, and among them peasants, whom he regarded as good and interesting people, and he was continually observing new points in them, altering his former views of them and forming new ones" (Part 3, Chapter 1).

Tolstoy then proceeds to describe how Levin took his place with the peasants when they harvested the fields. He swung his scythe with them and partook of their humble meal at midday. Sergei Ivanovich Koznishev, on the other hand, the great champion of the "people," spent the whole morning in bed.

Finally, let it be noted that modern forms of slavery—those based on ethnic, racial, and religious differences—have no support in either Sirach or the rest of the Bible.

◦: SIRACH 34 :◦

This chapter covers two themes. The first is an instruction with respect to prudence (vv. 1–17), and the second introduces a longer treatment of the true worship of God (34:18—35:24).

In the first part, the instruction on prudence, Sirach treats of three subjects: a common-sense distrust of dreams (vv. 1–7), the confidence born of experience (vv. 8–11), and trust in the Lord (vv. 12–17).

With respect to dreams, Sirach's distrust seems singular in Holy Scripture. One recalls the several instances in biblical history where dreams are the medium used to reveal the divine will and plan. Most memorable in this respect are the accounts of the two Josephs, the Old Testament patriarch and the New Testament foster father of Jesus. It is ironical, moreover, that Sirach is almost a contemporary of the Book of Daniel, which says a great deal of the revelatory and prophetic value of dreams.

Sirach's approach to this subject, however, has more to do with prudence than with prophecy. He stresses what most common-sense people easily recognize—that it is normally imprudent, even foolish, to put much stock in dreams. There is a clear sense in which dreams are not *real* and should not be taken as real.

Indeed, the stories of Daniel and the two Josephs are special, in the sense of exceptional. Neither Daniel nor the two Josephs are ordinary men. On the contrary, with respect to their dreams, they are more to be admired than imitated.

While Sirach admits that God *can* and sometimes *does* reveal His counsel through a dream (v. 6), it is more often the case, he is convinced, that trusting in dreams leads to massive deception (v. 7).

In general, dreams are the projections of our hopes (v. 1), our fantasies (v. 2), our superficial associations (v. 3), and our personal fables (v. 4). Using them as a form of divination is sure to lead to folly (v. 5). It is far more prudent to base our confidence on the experience we gain while we are awake!

In gaining the confidence born of experience, Sirach especially recommends travel (vv. 9–11). Almost all educators appreciate the intellectual and moral advantages of travel, and Sirach makes this observation as the fruit of his personal experience.

That experience has also taught him the importance of trusting in God (vv. 12–17). It is difficult to argue with—and impossible to defeat—the person whose confidence is based on the experience of God's providential guidance and care over the years. This confidence, which far transcends any theory on the matter, can be trusted. Indeed, it is the height of prudence to do so.

The latter part of this chapter (vv. 18–26) is the beginning of a short treatise on worship (which lasts until 35:24). Among the Wisdom authors of Holy Scripture, Sirach is singular in his attention to worship. Indeed, the book itself is addressed to the man who "approaches to *serve the Lord*" (*prosecle doulevein Kyrio*, 2:1). For Sirach the service of God is the true life of man. Moreover, his book will culminate in a vivid description of the sacrificial worship of the Lord in the second temple.

Sirach's introduction of the theme of worship in this chapter follows logically on his preceding comments about remembering the Lord's providential care (vv. 13–17). It is this remembrance that prompts him to worship.

Sirach is inspired, furthermore, by the teaching of the prophets in his emphasis on the interior state of a man's soul in worship. Like Isaiah, he knows that worship can be a great escape from God, if it consists simply in the performance of ritual actions and the recitations of liturgical texts that are not believed and not taken seriously. Apart from the proper internal dispositions of faith, justice, and love, worship's outer ritual is only a form of mockery, and it is very dangerous to mock God.

Again like Isaiah, Sirach condemns any divorce of worship from man's moral responsibilities in society (vv. 18, 20). If these have not been met, man has no business appearing in the sight of the Almighty. There is no "atonement for sin" (*exsilasketai hamartias*) in the mere multiplying of sacrifices (v. 20). One thinks of very sinful men who have used ill-gotten money to provide that the Holy Eucharist will be offered for them for centuries to come. Sirach stands with Isaiah in his condemnation of a religion that imagines that God's displeasure can be "appeased" in this way.

What is the Lord more likely to hear, asks Sirach, the prayers of the man who steals the bread of the poor, or the curses of the poor man whose bread was stolen (v. 24)?

In short, a man does not come before God as an isolated individual. He is never "alone with the Alone." The man who continues to hate or defraud his neighbor can never truly worship God.

Sirach touches here on a problem with worship that has been with us from the beginning. Who can fail to recall that the world's first murder was conceived in the act of worship? "Now in the process of time Cain brought a sacrifice to the Lord from the fruits of the ground. Abel also brought a sacrifice from the firstborn of his flock and of their fat. The Lord respected Abel and his offering, but He did not respect Cain and his sacrifices. So Cain was extremely sorrowful, and his countenance fell" (Genesis 4:3–5). God did not receive the worship of Cain because there was something seriously wrong with Cain's heart. Cain was an unbelieving, hardhearted, and hateful man, and these sentiments would soon be expressed in the murder of his brother. This is the problem in worship observed by Isaiah and Sirach.

Is it not significant that Luke, the New Testament writer who says most about prayer, is also the one who says the most about taking care of the poor?

There is a genuine sense in which an individual can flee to worship as an escape from his moral ties to humanity. He can use the time of prayer as a means of eluding the censures of his conscience. Thus, Jesus warned against bringing our sacrifice to the altar before we are reconciled with our brother. Such was the failure of Cain.

~: SIRACH 35 :~

This chapter continues the theme of correct worship begun in the preceding. In that chapter Sirach took pains to maintain the unity of worship with social responsibility. This same preoccupation inspires him in the present chapter as well.

Our author begins by equating worship with other aspects of the devout life: observance of the Torah (v. 1), reciprocation and almsgiving (v. 2), and eschewing evil (v. 3). Such things, he says, are equal to the four types of temple sacrifice that he mentions here.

Such an equation was surely influenced by Israel's experience in captivity just a few centuries earlier. During their forty years of exile in Babylon the Jews, deprived of the temple and its daily ritual sacrifices, had learned to substitute other forms of sacrifice. They had taken to heart the warnings of Isaiah and the other eighth-century prophets, who had insisted that the Lord required more than the mere observance of an external ritual. What God really sought, they came to see, were "the weightier matters of the Law: justice and mercy and faith" (Matthew 23:23). These could take the place of the prescribed sacrifices (cf. Augustine, *The City of God* 10.5). Sirach here incorporates that insight into his theology of worship.

At the same time, Sirach is no opponent of the temple ritual, as we shall see when he comes to describe it in chapter 50. Even in the present chapter, the references to the altar and its sacrifices (vv. 6–11, 16) should probably be understood literally.

Nonetheless, the worshipper should never imagine that the just God can be "bought off" with ritual sacrifice (v. 12). Only the sacrifice of a just man is acceptable to the Lord (v. 6). An unjust man should expect God to attend, rather, to the prayers of the poor against those who oppress them (vv. 13–15).

The final verses of this chapter (vv. 17–24) may have in mind the sufferings of the Chosen People under Greco/Syrian domination at the end of the third and through the opening decades of the second century before Christ, roughly from the accession of Antiochus III in 223 BC until the rededication of the second temple in 165. The prayer of the poor man, in this case, is the petition of Israel for redress against its oppressors. Such a prayer becomes, in turn, an implicit plea for the sending of the Messiah. Sirach offers such a prayer in the following chapter.

⌁ SIRACH 36 ⌁

This chapter has two parts, the first (vv. 1–17) containing a long, solemn prayer, and the second (vv. 18–26) an admonition on the choice of friends.

In the previous chapter Sirach finished with comments on the efficacy of the prayers of the oppressed. Now he provides a lengthy example (vv. 1–17).

Surely this is not a general prayer. The author has in mind, rather, the current state of oppressed Jews. Thus, we note that the prayer comes from the first person plural, "us" and "we." It is "the people" who are oppressed (v. 9).

Indeed, were it not for the internal evidence indicating that the book was finished by 180 BC, one would be disposed to date this prayer in the context of the persecution of the Jews by Antiochus IV Epiphanes, especially his defilement of the second temple in December of 167.

This latter persecution, however, was the culminating offense in a long period of strife and infidelity, as we know from the books of Maccabees.

At this period, evil, self-serving Jews had already defiled the holiness required of God's people by their complicity with the pagans that dominated the western end of the Fertile Crescent. These Jews had compromised with the Greco-Syrian culture of the day. This latter is what Sirach appears to be describing when he speaks of "the strange nations" (vv. 1–4). These are the proud heathens that despise Israel (v. 10).

Sirach prays that the Lord will renew the wonders He wrought of old, new forms of the ancient punishments He had visited on Egypt (v. 6; cf. Ezekiel 20:41).

Sirach asks that the time until retribution be shortened (v. 8). He looks for the appointed hour of deliverance, the age of the Messiah. We have here one of the very few places an apocalyptic theme is found in the Bible's Wisdom literature.

Germane to this theme is the gathering of scattered Israel

(v. 11). Although the Persian policies of repatriation had permitted the Jews to return to the Holy Land in the late sixth century, rather few had actually done so. Meanwhile other Jews had migrated to Egypt and Abyssinia, and an increasing number of them had settled in the Fertile Crescent and around the shores of the Mediterranean. By this time far more Jews lived outside the Holy Land than within it. This internationalizing of the Chosen People, their effective separation from the land that defined them, substantially altered the Jewish religion.

Sirach is not among those who considered this a good thing. He wanted a restoration of things as they had been "from the beginning" (vv. 11, 15). This gathering of the scattered would be the fulfillment of prophecy (vv. 15–16). Sirach's prayer was answered in due course, when Caiaphas declared, "You know nothing at all, nor do you consider that it is expedient for us that one man should die for the people, and not that the whole nation should perish." This declaration was tied specifically to the prayer of Sirach, because Caiaphas did not say this "on his own authority; but being high priest that year he prophesied that Jesus would die for the nation, and not for that nation only, but also that He would gather together in one the children of God who were scattered abroad" (John 11:49–52).

The latter part of this chapter (vv. 18–26) begins a new topic that will preoccupy Sirach into the next chapter (through 37:6). This is the theme of a person's social relationships, his friends, spouse, associates, and counselors.

Sirach's interest in this subject is consonant with his view that the pursuit of wisdom not only takes place in a social context, but is at every point related to that context. As we have hitherto reflected so often, the wise man strives for wisdom, not as an isolated seeker, but with a cultivated moral sense of his duties and place in society. He pursues wisdom as essential to his social responsibilities.

These responsibilities chiefly concern the domestic setting—a man's duties as a son, a brother, a husband, a father, and a grandfather—but they also involve his life in the larger social setting, an important aspect of which is friendship. Such is the concern addressed in this section of the book. He treats this concern with a series of aphorisms.

A first consideration is trust, concerning which our author

appeals to the metaphor of taste. Much as a man discerns what sort of food he has in his mouth by the taste of it, he says, so gradually a man learns to distinguish the moral character of the man who is speaking with him (vv. 18–19). "The heart understands deceptive words"—*kardia synete logous pseudeis* (my translation).

Doubtless this discernment takes some time to acquire, but the acquisition of it is essential to moral responsibility. It is morally irresponsible to place trust in an undeserving person, and not all men speak the truth. Hence, not all men are to be trusted. The wise man must learn to determine which ones.

What is said of men seems doubly true of women, in Sirach's opinion. In respect to women, after all, men are in need of more discernment, because the heart is more disposed to be deceived (vv. 21–23). Indeed, hardly any relationship seems more vulnerable to deception than that between the sexes.

This concern especially pertains to a man's choice of a wife, on which choice so much of his future happiness depends (vv. 24–25). It is obviously of great importance that a person is not deceived in the choice of a spouse.

Finally, says Sirach, only that man is to be trusted who shows signs of stability. A vagabond is always suspect, because he is arguably a rootless person (v. 26).

∾ SIRACH 37 ∾

This chapter may be divided into four parts, of which the first continues the theme of friendship from the previous chapter (vv. 1–6), the second contains advice on the choice of counselors (vv. 7–15), the third stresses the need for prudent counsel (vv. 16–26), and the last gives an exhortation to temperance (vv. 27–31).

In continuity with the subject of chapter 36, Sirach first turns to the loyalty expected in a friend. He gives several reasons for caution in this regard.

First, most men describe themselves as a "friend" of somebody or other. Hardly any noun is more readily used in self-description, but that fact points to the problem. In the use of this word, especially in self-descriptions, a particular kind of Nominalism sets in, because a friend may be an *onomati monon philos*, "a friend in name only" (v. 1). What is sought in friendship, however, is Realism; we all want the *res*, the genuine article.

Truth to tell, it is far better to have a determined enemy than a friend who becomes an enemy (v. 2; 6:9). This is the kind of enemy who can do us the most harm. Job knew about this kind of friendship, as did the Psalmist, but the Bible's chief example is Judas Iscariot, who embodies the very name "traitor." Such a one covers the earth with deceit (v. 3).

Not so bad as this, but not a great deal better, is the unreliable friend. While he may not turn traitor, he proves himself unworthy of trust when the times turn difficult. Such a one is less a *philos*, a friend, than a *hetairos*, an associate (OSB, "companion," v. 4). He maintains a sort of friendship when friendship is convenient to him, but not much longer. Since someone may unwisely depend on him, however, his insouciance to the duties of friendship will become a form of opposition (*apenanti*).

It is wise, in the choice of friends, to be acquainted with their motives. It will not take very long to discern whether a potential friend is really acting out of self-interest.

What is said of friends is especially important in the choice of counselors. Be cautious, says Sirach, about trusting a person who gives advice because he simply likes to give advice (v. 7). Especially be careful not to reveal your disadvantages to such a one, because he may be seeking only to further his own cause at your expense. It is not likely that his counsel will be disinterested. Wise men do not reveal their weaknesses to someone likely to take advantage of them (vv. 9–10).

Some people, on the other hand, simply cannot be trusted on certain particular subjects. Be particularly careful, says Sirach, when speaking with women who are jealous of one another, or with the fainthearted with respect to conflict, or with merchants with respect to the market, or with anyone when the subject of the discussion invites a conflict of interest (v. 11).

Godly men, however, make the best friends and counselors (v. 12). If a man is loyal to God, he can be trusted in other matters.

A wise man gradually learns to trust the instincts of his own heart with respect to the presence of danger (vv. 13–14). He leaves an inheritance of wisdom, not only during his lifetime, but for the entire history of Israel (v. 25). This is salvation history, and the wise man contributes to the tradition that is the substance of that history. Coming generations will be instructed from his teaching.

Sirach here reflects what was happening in biblical history itself, because the third part of the Hebrew Bible, the *Ketubim* or *Writings*, was gradually being added to the Bible during that period. The age of the Torah and the age of the prophetic writings had come to an end; this was the age of the "Scribes," such as Ezra and the Chronicler, whose writings would soon become part of the biblical canon.

In everything concerning Wisdom, we first give ourselves over to prayer (v. 15).

For all the difficulty of finding dependable counselors, however, counsel itself is of extreme importance in every significant undertaking (vv. 16–26).

This recourse is dictated by prudence, the practical application of discernment in the decisions and enterprises that go to make up human life (v. 16). In this verse our author places counsel (*boule*) in parallel with reason (*logos*). All practical human activity must meet the standards of counsel and reason, because precipitous decisions rarely lead to success, and constant recourse to spontaneity is the mark of a fool.

Inimical to the practice of prudent consultation is excessive indulgence in speech (vv. 17–18). When we look for a wise person to guide us, says Sirach, it is better to avoid the man who is too quick to give advice (v. 19). He has in mind here the man learned in many subjects, but none of them profitable to his own soul (*he idia psyche*).

There is another type of counselor who uses all the right words (*en logois*), but in fact he lacks the grace that comes from the Lord (*para Kyriou charis*). He will not be profitable as a counselor (vv. 20–21).

Finally, having discussed prudence, Sirach turns to temperance, or self-control (vv. 27–31). In his discussion of gluttony and related subjects, we observe that he is less concerned with the spiritual harm attendant on these vices than with the danger they pose to a person's physical health. These reflections prepare for his comments about physicians in the next chapter.

∾: SIRACH 38 :∾

This chapter has three parts. The first (vv. 1–15) is devoted to care of one's health and the dignity of the physician's art, the second (vv. 16–23) is a consideration of death, and the third (vv. 24–34) begins a longer discussion about the relative merit of various vocations.

The previous chapter had closed with some counsel on temperance and the proper control of diet. We observed that the motive given for such discipline was not so much the good of the soul but rather the proper maintenance of the body. Sirach's explicit concern, that is to say, was for good health and the avoidance of disease. He continues this concern in the present chapter, where he considers both sickness and death.

Sirach begins with the honor and importance of the physician (vv. 1–3, 13) and the value of medicine (vv. 4–8). Of the physician he says, "the Lord created him" (*avton ektisen Kyrios*). Since the only true healer is God, it follows that the physician mediates the divine blessing of restoration to health (v. 2). Consequently, the physician is properly someone to be held in honor (v. 3).

To us, of course, these sentiments are obviously expected, but that appreciation for the physician was not necessarily shared by Sirach's contemporaries. For example, writing not so terribly long before Sirach, the Chronicler had spoken critically of King Asa, who in illness had "sought physicians rather than the Lord" (2 Chronicles 16:12). Clearly, the Chronicler had no high regard for the healing arts.

Sirach's attitude in this matter is radically different and strikes the modern reader as more advanced and enlightened. There is a genuine sense in which this assessment is true, of course.

Sirach, in his respect for the physician's skills, could not convincingly appeal to the ancient traditions embodied in Holy Scripture. For instance, if he sought in those sources an example of the salubrious effects of plants, he could not find much other than the tree that sweetened the bitter water (v. 5; cf. Exodus 15:22–25; 2 Kings

2:19–22). Not much is said in the Old Testament about the virtues of medicine.

In fact, medicinal healing was not one of those arts in which the Jew enjoyed a distinction over the Persian, the Egyptian, or the Greek. The study and practice of the healing arts pertain, rather, to the more general sciences, which do not so directly benefit from special revelation.

Consequently, in affirming the honor of the physician, Sirach somewhat steps out of his role as a Jewish apologist and takes a place at the more common human table of science—here the science of medicine—as a gift from God. Which is to say, the Lord *created* the physician. Medicine is among those divine gifts—like sunshine and rain—of which Jesus says that they are given equally to both the sinner and the righteous. Certain of God's blessings do not consult the moral state of the recipients. Drugs and remedies work pretty much equally on the just and unjust.

In this respect we may perhaps speak of a kind of "humanism" in Sirach, expressed in a sympathy for human achievement in the field of medicine and healing. If today we take this sympathy for granted, it is worth remembering the first time it appears in biblical literature.

Having spoken of prayers for the sick (v. 14), Sirach next turns his attention to concern for the dead (vv. 16–23). Although these themes are not related by logic, they are certainly related in common experience.

Care for the dead is arguably the best general indicator of the cultural values and expectations of any society. If we compare, for example, the very different ways in which the Etruscans and the Romans treated the remains of their departed, we discern the profound cultural change that took place in Italy when the Romans became ascendant over the Etruscans: Etruscans buried the remains of their dead, and the Romans cremated them. These variant practices testified to two different views of existence. Much the same contrast must be noted in the ascendancy of Islam over Zoroastrianism in the history of Persia: Muslims bury their dead, whereas Zoroastrians leave their bodies to be consumed by carnivorous birds. These two practices testify to two radically different schools of metaphysics.

In the Bible—in both Testaments—the proper treatment of the

dead is burial. Indeed, according to Holy Scripture the surest way of desecrating a dead body is to burn it. This fact indicates the enormous cultural gulf separating Israel from Greece to the west and India to the east. It points to a dozen ways in which biblical cosmology differs from Hellenic and Hindu cosmologies. Biblical man—in both Testaments—believed the human person to be inseparable from his body. Belief in the resurrection of the body—such as we see in 2 Maccabees 7—represented the high point of the Old Testament hope, which the Christian faith was happy to affirm (Hebrews 11:35; Acts 2:32, 36; 13:31–32; 24:14–15).

It is a fact that the preaching of the Gospel throughout Greco-Roman civilization immediately led to the adoption of burial by peoples that had earlier practiced cremation. Indeed, cemeteries are arguably the earliest physical expression of that culture's acceptance of the Gospel—earlier than church buildings, earlier than monasteries, earlier than shrines. As far as we can tell, the first real estate ever owned by Christian congregations was set aside for burial grounds. Christians had catacombs in Rome before they ever had church buildings.

Burial and cremation—to limit our considerations to just these two—are radically different cultural proclamations. Each practice is based on a different cosmology, even a different metaphysics. A change in the way a people treats dead bodies always means a change in religion, even when other aspects of a culture stay the same. How any society treats its dead is the deepest indication of what it believes about existence. If Christians ever start to cremate bodies—in such a way that it becomes a general and normal expectation—it will be only a short time before they lose their faith in the resurrection of the body. They will be calling themselves Christians, but behaving like Hindus. They will, in due course, adopt a Hindu view of existence; there will be scarcely any difference between Jesus and Vishnu.

Sirach, who is most zealous to maintain the values and principles inherited in Israel, is understandably conservative with respect to the dead. He insists on the proper observance of all the rituals associated with a decent mourning and burial (v. 16; cf. Jeremiah 9:7; Amos 5:6; Ezekiel 24:15–24; Acts 9:36–39). He encourages appropriate expressions of grief; for him the loss of a loved one is not the proper occasion for restraint and self-control. Although the proper mourning period at that time was a week (cf. 22:12), the first day or so, Sirach says, must be especially intense (v. 17).

After that, however, Sirach encourages a speedy return to normal life, because the dead do not benefit from the tears shed over them, and too much grief is not good for the human spirit. Sirach warns against a sorrow unreasonably extended (vv. 19–23).

The final portion of this chapter (vv. 24–34) is the first section of a new theme that runs to 39:11. This theme is a comparison of, and contrast between, the vocations of the scribe and the craftsman. While Sirach understandably prefers the calling of the scribe, which is his own (39:1–11), he also shows respect for the skill and wisdom of the craftsman, on whom depends the stability and prosperity of the city. This chapter describes the labor of craftsmen.

There was an enhanced division of labor in Sirach's society. He speaks here of the farmer and the raiser of livestock (vv. 25–26), the carpenter and the engraver (v. 27), the metal worker (v. 28), and the potter (vv. 29–30). The good estate of society requires and rewards all these skills. Indeed, the cultivation of these crafts separates a civilized society from barbarism.

Moreover, these crafts provide the leisure essential to the reflection and studies of the scribe (v. 24). The long hours and consequent fatigue of the laborer (vv. 25, 27, 28, 30) render him unfit to engage in scribal pursuits, which require adequate leisure and freedom to think, reflect, and study. The very term "school" comes from *schole*, the Greek word meaning "leisure." It is a mark of civilized society that it provides the young with the freedom and means to become educated. Ideally, youth is especially the time for study.

Even as he contrasts the varying labors of the scribe and the craftsman, however, we don't find in Sirach the signs of disrespect and disparagement obvious in other authors who elaborated the same contrast. The tone of Sirach is a far cry from "The Instruction of Duauf" (Pritchard, *Ancient Near Eastern Texts*, pp. 432–434), in which an ancient Egyptian scribe poked fun at the miserable lives of non-intellectuals. Sirach's respectful tone is closer to Hesiod's *Works and Days*.

In the light of the rabbinic tradition as a whole, Sirach's reflections on this concern will seem an anomaly unless we regard him as simply expressing one side of a practical problem. Judaism as a whole, after all, was reluctant to free the rabbi from the skills and practice of manual labor. As evidenced in the life of the rabbinic tentmaker Paul, it was common for scribes and scholars to maintain the skills of the practical crafts and even to make their living thereby. Judaism was careful not to separate its intellectuals from the working class, its scribes from its artisans.

Even as the latter practice prevailed, nonetheless, Sirach's reflections gave voice to a common concern, a concern shared by Paul. He too recognized that his scribal skills, his work as a religious instructor, theoretically justified the reception of a proper maintenance, quite apart from his manual labor (cf. 1 Corinthians 9:4–11).

The problem noted by Sirach and Paul has never been completely resolved, though in practice the Christian Church generally recognizes that a teacher or pastor is better able to serve in that vocation if he is set free from the necessity of making a living by some other means. The monastic vocation has been less unanimous on the point, some monastic traditions insisting that monks be supported by the labor of their hands, not by their teaching, writing, or intellectual work.

~: SIRACH 39 :~

This chapter is divided into two parts. The first (vv. 1–11), which completes a contrast begun in the previous chapter, is a description of the life of the scribe, Sirach's own vocation. The second (vv. 12–35) is a praise of the divine wisdom manifest in Creation, with special consideration given to the existence of evil.

In his picture of the scribe's vocation (vv. 1–11), we observe Sirach's attention to history and literature. To understand the vocation of the biblical scribe one must grasp the content of his study. For the biblical wise man, the proper object of study is the inheritance he has received from the past.

We may contrast Sirach's view with the approach of those philosophers who thought according to the models of Socrates and the Buddha, both of whom began philosophy with the study of the soul. The biblical wise man does not start with the study of his soul, but with the study of Israel's history and literature, of which the central and formative part is the Torah.

If we look in the philosophical traditions of the pagan world for some possible parallel to the approach of Sirach, perhaps the closest would be that of Confucius, according to whom the pursuit of wisdom commenced with the study of China's cultural and historical inheritance. Confucius was very different, in this respect, from the Chinese philosopher Lao Tzu, who began, not with memory and history, but with consciousness in the present.

In making the pursuit of wisdom identical with the study of history, Sirach is preparing the reader for the long finale of his book—the praise of famous men.

In the opening verse we have our first outline of biblical literature, which is said to consist of the Torah, the Prophets, and the Wisdom literature. Sirach recognizes the deep, parabolic mysteries contained in this material (vv. 2–3).

Indeed, although the travels of the scribe (v. 4) may refer to actual geography, the verse may also connote the kind of travel that is done by the serious reader of inspired literature. That is to say, travel can take place in time as well as in space, and the stories in the Bible certainly provide "travel through strange countries."

Such study, nonetheless, is inseparable from the life of prayer and repentance (v. 5). The scribe's vocation, according to Sirach, is not the self-indulgent life of the dilettante. Prayer is both the source and the final fruit of his study (v. 6).

By the prayerful pursuit of this study, a man becomes part of the history on which his spirit feeds (vv. 7–11).

In the second part of this chapter (vv. 12–35) Sirach offers an example of the scribe's reflections—the contemplation of divine wisdom in Creation.

Sirach is quietly commencing the historical outline that will give structure to the rest of the book. Here he starts with Creation; in the next chapter he will take up the theme of man's Fall and the evils resulting from that tragedy.

Here we have Creation. Although this is a hymn of praise to the Creator, our author uses it as the setting to consider the classical problem encountered by theodicy: how to explain the manifest presence of evil in a world that owes its existence to an all-good and almighty God. The presence of such evil is a matter of experience; the persuasion of it rests on empirical evidence, from which there is no flight. Against persuasion stands the mind's conviction that all things outside of God owe their existence to God.

The antithesis between the former evidence and the latter conviction poses the sort of philosophical problem to which the scribe must apply the workings of his mind, and we recall that it was addressed at length in the Book of Job. Now Sirach turns his thoughts to this subject, confessing that he has given the problem much thought (vv. 12, 32).

Like the Book of Job, Sirach incorporates this problem into a praise of divine wisdom. His treatment of the subject, that is to say, is explicitly doxological. This is not surprising, since he has already indicated that the scribe's life of study is a life of prayer (vv. 5, 8). He begins, then, by praising God for the wisdom and goodness of His works (vv. 13–16), much as we find in the final part of the Psalter and in the song of Daniel's three young men in the furnace.

In the midst of this praise, Sirach suddenly reflects on man's sinful disposition to ask skeptical questions about purpose in the structure of the world (vv. 17, 21). Whereas the devout mind sees a moral reason for the presence of harm and evil in Creation (vv. 22, 23, 25), this truth is hidden from the unrepentant (v. 24). So far as they serve God's intention, all created things are good. One aspect of God's intention, however, is to punish and restrain the evildoer, and this latter is certainly not disposed to see goodness in all that God does (v. 27).

Thus, the destructive phenomena of nature, such as perilous weather (v. 29), dangerous animals, and the hazards of war (v. 30), reveal the righteous wrath of God toward the unrepentant (vv. 28, 30).

Sirach does not think of this negative aspect of Creation merely in terms of divine punishment, however, but also in terms of divine warning. Sirach was not a foolish or shallow man; he knew very well that the obvious evils in life—perilous weather, dangerous animals, the hazards of war, and so forth—are roughly common to all human beings, with scant regard to their moral state. Many tragedies of life are suffered by the righteous as well as the wicked, and only a very unobservant person would imagine otherwise.

Sirach's insight is deeper than this. He makes no attempt to reconcile good and evil in an abstract way. When he regards the presence of evil in the world, he does not consider it *in se*, but only *quoad nos*—not abstractly but in terms of human experience. According to Sirach's completely existential approach, even evil is included among those things of which he sings, "*All* things are the works of the Lord, / For they are exceedingly good" (39:16).

And what is evil's benefit to man? As Sirach sees the matter, the destructive side of this world inserts in the human mind a keener sense of God's moral resolve. The presence of peril encourages the cultivation of an honest conscience, honing a sharper edge on man's faculty of moral choice. The existence of evil, in short, places before man's eyes the fear of the Lord, which is the beginning of wisdom.

To appreciate Sirach's insight here, we may consider what our experience would be without the moral stimulus of circumambient evil. Had the merciful Creator not placed in His handiwork its harmful components, man would have far less incentive to mature as a moral being. The existence of evil inspires in the human soul a moral challenge, and this challenge is an essential part of God's word to man in the very structure of the created world.

ᵉ: SIRACH 40 :ᵕ

This chapter has three parts. First, having dealt with God's Creation in the previous chapter, our author now moves on to man's Fall (vv. 1–11). Second, he insists that in the created universe, which is still a just place in spite of the Fall, there continues to be a moral struggle between good and evil in history (vv. 12–17). Third, our author meditates on the joys of life in this world and how to preserve them (vv. 18–30).

In the section on the Fall (vv. 1–11), Sirach begins by lamenting the trials endured by human beings, which come from man's fall from grace in Genesis 3: "Hard work was created for every man / And a heavy yoke for the sons of Adam, / From the day they come forth from their mother's womb / until the day they return to the mother of all" (v. 1). This assessment of the human prospect is drawn directly from Genesis 3:19: "In the sweat of your face you shall eat bread till you return to the ground from which you were taken."

The chief and final punishment of sin is death at the end of a troublesome life. The knowledge of this inevitable fate darkens men's thoughts throughout their whole lives (v. 2). No matter their state and social standing in life, all men are subject to the fate of death (vv. 3–4).

Sirach lists seven afflictions that burden man during the day, before he climbs into bed for a bit of rest (v. 5), during which he suffers from bad dreams (vv. 6–7). This number, seven, is the symbol of perfection, in this case meaning that man is *perfectly* miserable! All these evils have come from the first sin, to which all subsequent sinners have added their contribution of evil (vv. 8–9).

Finally, having summarized the effects of sin, Sirach comes to the Deluge: "All these things were created for the lawless, / And because of them the flood came" (v. 10).

This mention of the flood prepares for the next section (vv. 12–17), where the created world is described as a place where God recognizes the difference between good and evil in men's lives.

The major message in these verses is the thesis that God does not bless evil. Thus, while bribery and injustice may bring about a temporary advantage, they do not have the blessing of God and will in the end be destroyed. Honesty, though it may suffer in the short run, will at the end stand forever (v. 12). Unjust wealth will last no longer than a thunderclap (v. 13).

Generosity, in which a man endeavors to imitate God, normally brings happiness to the giver (v. 14), and almsgiving brings an everlasting reward (v. 17).

All these aphorisms are based on Sirach's intuitive identification of the good with the permanent. No good can be lost or done in vain, because it invites the blessing of God.

The deep moral purpose at the base of life is not to be identified with any aspect of Creation as such, but it comes from God's providential influence on history. It is Sirach's conviction that God is never on the side of evil. As Lord of history, He is able to bring good out of evil, as we see in the ancient saga of Joseph, but God never takes the side of evil against good.

And this is the reason for the final triumph of good over evil. Wisdom consists in taking the same side God takes.

Having considered the miseries attendant on man's Fall (vv. 1–11) and the punishment that awaits evil behavior (vv. 12–17), Sirach now turns his thought to the modest but real joys available to the prudent, discerning man who will work for them (vv. 18–30). These joys are not everything, but neither are they nothing. They are the simple blessings of God generally given to those who live in righteousness.

Sirach considers them in a series of ten comparisons, in which the thematic word is "better" (vv. 18–26). Thus, while life is sweet for the man who works hard, it is even better for one who discovers an unexpected treasure (v. 18). Although it is no small thing to have a city named for you, a virtuous wife is a better blessing (v. 19). Wine and song are great, says Sirach, but the "love of wisdom" (*agapesis sophias*) is better (v. 20). And so forth.

The ten comparisons are not contrasts. They simply point to an order among things that are good. Some goods are more to be valued than others. A good singing voice, for instance, is better than skill with a musical instrument (v. 21). The actual shoots on an edible plant are better than other things that merely look good (v. 22). A husband and wife together are better than two friends (v. 23), and sound advice is beyond the price of precious metals (v. 24).

These comparisons represent a refinement of practical moral wisdom. The young man should be trained to recognize not only the difference between good and evil, but also the difference between good and better.

We observe that, among good things, Sirach places a higher value on things less tangible and physical, when these are of a more spiritual nature. Thus, sound counsel and the love of wisdom are manifestly superior to material things, and the fear of the Lord is the highest of all (vv. 26–27).

Sirach finishes by an exhortation against begging (vv. 28–30). This is a practical warning to the young, not the outline of a social program. The Bible has no objection to begging in principle. The present context considers begging only in the case of the person who would choose to beg rather than provide for himself. That is to say, what is being condemned here is the actual choice of begging as a preferred lifestyle.

❦ SIRACH 41 ❧

This chapter falls into three distinct parts. The first of these is a very brief reflection on death (vv. 1–4), the second a meditation on the historical fate of the wicked (vv. 5–14), and the third (which extends into the next chapter) a consideration of the theme of shame (41:15—42:8).

In his brief reflection on death, Sirach comments on a point that comes often to observation—namely, death does not always appear in the same guise. When it suddenly befalls a healthy man in full possession of his powers and at peace with his existence, death appears as a cruel and bitter intruder. It is distressing even to remember death in such circumstances (v. 1). On the other hand, when death visits the old and failing, it may take on the guise of a deliverer.

Arguably the most famous interpretation of these first two verses is found in the third song of the *Vier Ernste Gesänge* ("Four Serious Songs"), a collection that Johannes Brahms composed for piano and one baritone.

The third song consists of five parts, which render an interpretation of Sirach's two considerations of death: a bitter intruder or welcome deliverer. These two themes of Sirach are embodied in the two halves of Brahms's song: The first part is about the bitterness of death when it befalls otherwise happy people. The second half of the song, which shifts to a more robust E major, speaks of death as a blessing for those less fortunate in life.

Gustav Ophüls, in his *Memories of Johannes Brahms*, describes the first performance of this piece at Pentecost in 1896. He especially observed the composer's intense reaction to these two verses of Sirach: "The third song, 'O death, how bitter thou art,' plainly gripped him so strongly during its delivery, that during the quiet close, 'O death, acceptable is thy sentence,' great tears rolled down his cheeks, and he virtually breathed these last words of the text, with a voice nearly choked with tears. I shall just never forget the moving impression of this song."

One is surely correct in supposing that this text of Sirach, as expressed in the haunting music of Brahms, prepared the composer's soul for death eleven months later.

According to Sirach, death is not to be feared, because it expresses a divine decree (v. 3; cf. Genesis 3:19). A wise man, then, accepts death as a duty he owes to God. It is to be the object of neither fear nor complaint.

In the second section of this chapter, Sirach's meditation on the historical fate of the wicked (vv. 5–14), he begins by observing that moral evil tends to be a patrimony: wicked parents rather often have wicked children (vv. 5–6). Such children, he says, have a right to complain of their parents (v. 7).

On the other hand, there are wicked children born of good parents. Raised under God's Law, they choose to forsake that inheritance. Given the larger argument developed in this book, Sirach may have in mind here those seduced by the surrounding pagan culture that was threatening the Jews of the time. Those who succumb to this temptation he likens to the fallen Adam and Eve (vv. 9–10).

When Sirach declares, "the evil name of sinners will be blotted out" (v. 11), he expresses a sentiment commonly whispered at the funerals of the wicked—namely, that some people's lives are best forgotten. This sentiment may not be invariably charitable, but it is often true. The memory of some men is so offensive that we feel disposed never to think of them again. They deserve no remembrance on the earth, nor a single moment in anyone's recollection. Besides eternal damnation, this is about the worst historical fate that can befall a man.

A good name, on the other hand, is worthy of a long remembrance (vv. 12–13). This is the reason the Church maintains the annual feast days of the saints. The just are held in everlasting remembrance.

The final section of this chapter (vv. 14–27) is the first half of a consideration about shame. In this first half, Sirach lists the occasions when it is appropriate to feel shame. In the next chapter, he will tally those times when shame is not appropriate.

Shame, as man's response to disappointed social expectations, is not always appropriate, much less helpful. On the one hand, social expectations help to give shape to the conscience; indeed, Henri Bergson calls them one of "two sources of conscience." In the measure that such expectations come from an inherited tradition of moral wisdom, they are, of course, very valuable. In Israel's oldest Wisdom literature, chiefly exemplified in the Book of Proverbs, we have the distillation of that social tradition. In this case, social expectations can speak to the conscience with authority. Shame comes from the disappointment of those expectations.

On the other hand, Sirach knows that many of his own contemporaries, having forsaken that ancient moral tradition of Israel, encourage social expectations of their own, which are very different. They too are able to inflict shame, however, and the young man must know how to assess that shame. Sirach will deal with this problem in the next chapter.

He begins his consideration of shame with an ironic contrast between a wise man and a fool (v. 15). When the two are usually contrasted, it is to the advantage of the wise man and the ridicule of the fool. This is what we normally expect. Hence, our surprise at suddenly finding a circumstance in which the fool is preferred to the wise man: "A man who hides his foolishness is better," says Sirach, "than a man who hides his wisdom" (v. 15). In this case the fool is shrewd enough not to let everyone know he is foolish! Sirach seems to be pointing this irony at himself, indicating that he has in hand a bit of wisdom which it would be inappropriate for him to hide (v. 16).

When, then, is it appropriate to feel shame? Sirach begins with man's first social authority: his parents. There are certain things, he says, that a man would be ashamed for his parents to know about him (v. 17). He follows by detailing those offenses for which shame is always appropriate: lawlessness, theft, dishonesty, unchastity, disrespect, and repeating gossip (vv. 18–27).

EXCURSUS:
Sirach and Ecclesiastes

The composer Brahms, when he aligned, in his *Vier Ernste Gesänge*, two texts from Ecclesiastes with one from Sirach, testified to a similarity between these two Wisdom authors, at least with respect to their attitudes towards death. This similarity prompts the biblical reader to compare Sirach and Ecclesiastes more closely.

The author of Ecclesiastes (in Hebrew *Qoheleth*, "preacher") seems to have written in the third century before Christ, perhaps a hundred years before Sirach. Like the author of Job (who was perhaps a bit earlier, as I argued in *The Trial of Job*), he subjected Israel's traditional approach to wisdom—the approach of Proverbs—to a very refined critique.

Ecclesiastes' most distinctive characteristic was what we may call a critical phenomenology. The noun in this expression means, in his case, that he endeavored only to say how things *looked* to him. He was careful never to say, in a dogmatic way, how things really *were*. If his book seems—as it surely does—more than slightly pessimistic, we would be doing him an injustice, I believe, to fault him for it. He was a phenomenologist, not a metaphysician. If we thought of him as a metaphysician, we would have to consider him a heretic!

Considering only the *appearance* of things, Ecclesiastes declared, I must say the whole business looks rather yucky and out of sorts. I would prefer, of course, to embrace with enthusiasm the jolly bright world of the Wisdom books to which I am heir, like the Book of Proverbs. Believe me, friends, that course would be fairer by far.

However, let me be perfectly honest, Ecclesiastes went on, the cheerful optimism espoused in Proverbs does not correspond with the plain and observable facts. Call me a pessimist, if you will, or even an existentialist, but I don't quite see that things necessarily turn out so rosy just because a man works hard from dawn to dusk, practices prudence and thrift at all times, controls his tongue and his passions, puts his trust in the Lord, and so on . . . Where was I? Oh, yes, I just don't see that all this effort will do him much good in the long run. It all seems rather pointless and a kind of chasing after wind. The entire business of life strikes me, rather, as a system of exercises in emptiness.

Such was the phenomenology of Ecclesiastes. But it was a "critical" phenomenology, in the sense that he really wasn't so sure about it. Life did not *always* appear to be so bleak. Not very often—but often enough to make him think twice about it—life looked pretty good. So Ecclesiastes took a *critical* approach to his own phenomenology. He was never dogmatic, even about his doubts.

After all, the appearance of life was forever changing. Though sometimes encouraging, existence mainly came up short of expectations. It was a better course, then, to try to get along without an optimistic theory which would, in the long run, prove disappointing. One should just take things as they *appeared*, but always second-guessing them—in short, a critical epistemology.

For Ecclesiastes, everything was *hebel*, a Hebrew word translated variously as "vanity," "wind," "emptiness," or "futility" (1:11). Indeed, this word *hebel* came from the same root as the name Abel, the famous just man who was also the first human being to get himself murdered. So much for being righteous.

This impression of emptiness pertains even to the pursuit of wisdom, Ecclesiastes believes (1:12–18; 2:12–17). He has experienced many sources of pleasure, but none of them, he has found, amount to much (2:1–11). Work isn't all that good either (2:18–26). And why waste so much effort to raise children? In the end, they will turn out how they want.

Will God's retribution set things straight in the afterlife? Don't count on it, Ecclesiastes warns, because these things are so uncertain (3:19–22, the text used by Brahms in the first of his *Serious Songs*). It may be the case, after all, that the dead are better off than we are, and perhaps the happiest of all are those that will never live (4:1–3, Brahms's second song). Two sure things there are, says Ecclesiastes: justice does not invariably prevail (7:15–18), and at the end there is only death (9:2–5). Meanwhile, he goes on, we may as well enjoy what little there is to enjoy (5:18; 11:9).

So what has Sirach to do with Ecclesiastes? Well, they are very similar in one respect: Unlike Proverbs, these two books present the reflections of individual authors, both of them post-exilic. These books show how Jewish wise men, familiar with the circum-ambient pagan philosophies of the time, addressed the substance of Israel's Wisdom tradition. In each case here, the reader is dealing with a real, personal mind, working out a philosophy of life in concrete circumstances of history.

On the other hand, these two authors—Sirach and Ecclesiastes—likewise show how wide apart such individual Jewish thinkers could be. One might almost think that Sirach (whom Melville, let us recall, thought far too depressing) had in mind to refute the pessimism of Ecclesiastes! Between the two of them, it was not a question of how to interpret a half-full or half-empty glass. Rather, Sirach saw a *full* glass, whereas Ecclesiastes saw a *broken* glass.

I carefully remarked that one might "almost" say Sirach was refuting Ecclesiastes. This was not quite the case, I think, because Sirach made no serious attempt to address that other writer's doubt about the afterlife. Sirach was simply unresponsive on the point, as perhaps a speculation too hazy to consider. Since he left that matter aside, Sirach's thought is vastly more optimistic than Ecclesiastes'.

Although Israel was rising to an explicit faith in the resurrection during that period (2 Maccabees 7:14; 12:43; LXX of Daniel 11:20), Sirach recorded no views on the point. A Christian must, of course, regard that silence as a serious theological deficiency. This is doubtless why Brahms added a fourth "serious song," which proclaimed: *Jetzt erkenne ich stückweise, dan aber werd ich erkennen, gleichwie ich erkennet bin*—"Now I know in part, but then I shall know just as I also am known."

❧ SIRACH 42 ❧

This chapter has three sections: The first (vv. 1–8) continues the theme of shame from chapter 41. The second (vv. 9–14) declares a father's duties to his household. The third (vv. 15–25) begins a long celebration of the divine glory manifest in the created world. This last will extend all through the following chapter and introduce Sirach's praise of famous men, the final part of the book.

The first section of the present chapter, which continues the theme of shame from the previous chapter, is devoted to those matters about which a man should *not* be ashamed, even when society expects him to be.

The first among these are the Torah and the Covenant (v. 2). Sirach wrote this exhortation in a context to which we have drawn attention several times: Many Jews, exposed to what appeared to be the more sophisticated standards of Hellenic culture, were truly embarrassed by their Jewish faith and inheritance. Thus, they gave in to an improper shame by reason of their inability to "fit in" and win acceptance from the prevailing paganism of the time. The pagans themselves had nothing but contempt for the Jewish Law and Covenant.

In that context Sirach was aware of a pronounced "generation gap," perhaps deeper than Israel had ever known. Parents now discovered that their children were actually ashamed of the Law and the Covenant. This problem brought about a genuine crisis within Palestinian Judaism, a crisis leading to the Maccabean revolt recorded in the Books of the Maccabees and the *Antiquities* of Flavius Josephus. Sirach's exhortation here should be read within the context of that emerging crisis.

A similar crisis was observed in early Christian history, when the Gospel was "to the Jews a stumbling block and to the Greeks foolishness" (1 Corinthians 1:23). It was "socially unacceptable" to adhere to the Gospel in those days, far more than is the case in our own society. It was that difficulty that Paul faced when he wrote to the Romans, "I am not ashamed of the gospel of Christ" (Romans 1:16).

It was in warning against such embarrassment that Jesus said, "Whoever is ashamed of Me and My words in this adulterous and sinful generation, of him the Son of Man also will be ashamed when He comes in the glory of His Father with the holy angels" (Mark 8:38). It was to that unworthy shame that Simon Peter succumbed when he denied knowing Jesus.

The man ashamed of God's Law, Sirach goes on, may become ashamed of other honorable things, such as generosity (v. 3), honesty (v. 4), prosperity, and the discipline of the home (v. 4). He elaborates these concerns, stressing the importance of security (v. 6), the proper maintenance of business records (v. 7), and the respect between the generations (v. 8). A man must not be ashamed of such things, no matter how unfashionable they may be.

In sum, then, a man who takes his moral guidance from social expectations does well in principle, but at the same time he should be cautious. Any society can lose its bearings and thereby lose its authority to address the conscience.

Sirach's comments about the discipline of the home (vv. 5–6) prompt him to add the second section of this chapter, a declaration of a man's duties to his household (vv. 9–14). This is the last such exhortation in the Book of Sirach. After it, our author will go immediately into his lengthy treatment of Creation and salvation history.

Among a man's domestic duties, according to Sirach, none is more arduous than the raising of daughters. They are a constant source of worry, anxiety, and sleepless nights. This problem never ceases, moreover, not even after the daughter is married and has become someone else's responsibility (v. 9). There are just so many different ways, Sirach laments, in which girls can go wrong.

Things started off on the wrong foot, he suggests, back with Eve, the first female to bring disgrace on her family, and things have not improved very much since then (v. 13).

It is hard enough, says Sirach, in the best of circumstances, but woe to the father whose daughter is stubborn and headstrong (v. 11). Over such a one a stricter watch must be kept. In a truly stubborn daughter a father may not safely place even the slightest trust.

A wise, prudent young woman, after all, is aware of her considerable vulnerabilities. She can be hurt in many more ways than a young man. Consequently, she will be cautious, which is exactly what a father hopes for.

A stubborn and foolish girl, on the other hand, is unable to recognize her vulnerability (or refuses to admit it, thinking it *unfair*), and this failure on her part renders her even more vulnerable—and dangerous. The last thing such a girl needs is an indulgent father. Her father may be the biggest safeguard standing between her and disaster.

Sirach probably had in mind the easier, less restrictive relationships between the sexes common in the Hellenic culture, which was such a great moral threat to Israel at that time. The Hellenic standards on this matter may have seemed attractive to young Jewish women.

Nonetheless, Sirach's caution on this subject seems extremely timely today, when the standards of the world—particularly the expectations of modern women—may easily prove a pitfall for young Christians.

The third and final part of this chapter (vv. 15–25) begins the last and longest section of the book: a lengthy praise of God for His works in Creation and salvation history (42:15—43:33), and the praise of those great historical figures through whom the divine wisdom guided the fortunes of God's people (44:1—51:30). This detailed historical survey renders the Book of Sirach unique in the Bible's Wisdom literature.

Beginning rather suddenly in the middle of the present chapter, Sirach's new theme breaks onto the scene with a measure of abruptness not much softened by its solemnity. In one breath our author laments the social problems occasioned by an evil woman (v. 14), and in the next breath he breaks forth into a long hymn of praise to God (v. 15).

This is one of the places in Holy Scripture where its division by chapters (an accomplishment we owe to Stephen Langton in the thirteenth century) is somewhat less than felicitous.

The unifying theme of this final part of Sirach was announced much earlier in the book—namely, divine wisdom resides in the people and institutions of Israel: "Then the Creator of all things commanded me, / And He who created me gave me a place to live. / He said, 'Pitch your tent in Jacob / And receive an inheritance in Israel'" (24:8). Such is the thesis to be argued in this last part of Sirach's work.

There are two further general observations to be made about this final part of Sirach:

First, he begins his historical survey with the created world itself, the physical setting where history takes place. He praises God's wisdom in the works of nature. In doing this, Sirach goes directly to the root of salvation history—namely, what God accomplished in the first six days of the world's existence. He goes to the opening chapter of Genesis.

In taking this approach, Sirach was hardly an innovator, because the inclusion of Creation among the divine deeds of salvation history was already characteristic of the Psalter. Psalm 88 (89), for example, places the entire Davidic covenant, the culminating covenant in the Hebrew Scriptures, within the mercy and truth by which God holds heaven and earth in being and balance. Or again, Psalms 134 and 135 (135 and 136), recounting the deliverance from Egypt and the conquest of the Promised Land, commence their narratives with the action of God in creating and sustaining the universe. The outline of Sirach's long hymn of praise, therefore, follows a standard narrative pattern exemplified in these and other psalms.

Second, in this final section Sirach forgoes all further moral exhortation and direct admonition. There are no more proverbs in this book, as the author turns entirely to poetry and storytelling. His purpose in this approach, however, is consistent with his polemical intention throughout the book: He has in mind to offer a compelling and attractive reason to prefer Israel's inherited wisdom to the Hellenic philosophy and culture that was so tempting to his countrymen, particularly the young.

Sirach starts with a general account of God's wisdom and power; then He goes on to show how these divine attributes are made visible in Creation (vv. 15–25). Sirach's thesis on this point is identical with that in the Wisdom of Solomon 13 and Romans 1: "For since the creation of the world His invisible *attributes* are clearly seen, being understood by the things that are made, *even* His eternal power and Godhead" (Romans 1:20).

In the Lord's words (*en logois Kyriou*), says Sirach, he can describe "His works" (*ta erga Avtou*, v. 15). The works Sirach has in mind are things that he sees (*ha heoraka*). He can see these things, he goes on, because of the light of the sun (v. 16). Not even the saints, nonetheless, can adequately describe the beauty of what God has made (v. 17).

Creation contains two abysses: the objective immeasurable space of the universe, and the subjective depths of the human heart (v. 18). These two infinities, inscrutable and beyond reckoning, call out to one another. Yet, God is able to take the measure of both (vv. 19–20).

Creation is not a jumble of different things, but a complete and integrated whole (*to pan*, v. 17)—a "*uni*-verse," in which each part is related to a single principle (vv. 24–25). This is all held together, says Sirach, by the Lord Almighty (*Kyrios ho Pantokrator*, v. 17).

~: SIRACH 43 :~

The praise of God in the works of Creation continues. Sirach began with the sun (42:16), because the sun's light is the necessary medium for seeing everything else. This fact places a radical irony within man's knowledge of material things—namely, the eye is so designed that it cannot gaze directly at its source of light without being destroyed by that light (*amavroi ophthalmous*, v. 4). The light is seen safely only when it is reflected on other objects.

This fact serves as a metaphor for the fundamental apophaticism of all human knowledge—namely, it is of the nature of truth that it makes *other things* true. The unaided mind cannot gaze at truth *in se*. It is known, rather, in the diverse things it enlightens. Like the priests who carried the Ark without looking into it, our minds run a serious risk when they try to evade that inbuilt epistemological restraint.

Sirach revels in the great diversity of objects on which the sun throws its light. He finds his delight in this diversity: the manifold colors revealed in the refraction of a single light.

Where should he begin his rehearsal of these wonders? He commences with the firmament, the overarching heavens, because that is where the sun resides and runs its course (v. 1).

This initial verse requires further grammatical comment. It is constructed of exactly nine words, eight of which are nouns. Having no verbal components at all, it is really not a sentence but a sort of exclamation. Its predications are accomplished entirely by the use of the genitive case and one preposition. Literally translated, the verse reads: "Summit of loftiness! Firmament of purity! Vision of heaven in contemplation of glory!"

Man begins his quest for wisdom by raising a contemplative gaze upwards to that pure and glorious vault, across which the sun runs its daily course. Before he turns his sight to the earth, Sirach lets it rest on the solemn serenity of the azure sky. He returns to the sun (v. 2), described here as the herald (*diangellon*—see the word "angel" here?) of the day, as it "goes forth" (*en exsodo*). Sirach especially concentrates on the heat of the sun (vv. 3–4). It is man's most primeval fire.

Sirach does not praise the sun, however, but the Lord who made it and sent it forth (v. 5).

The great contribution of the moon (vv. 6–8) is the regulation of the seasons and divisions of the months. Indeed, in all languages the words "month" and "moon" belong to the same root. The moon serves as the original sundial, by which man observes and measures the sequence of the days. In this sense the moon has been more "humanized" than the sun. The sun is likened to a furnace (*kamonon*, v. 4), whereas the moon is like a lamp, a "vessel encamped on high" (v. 8). Man uses the gentle moon to regulate the phases of his life.

As for the stars, they stand guard as sentinels in the heavens. They too serve the will of God (vv. 9–10).

Treating the heavenly bodies as works of God, the Bible takes its stand against idolatry. Not regarding the stars, planets, and moons as divine, Sirach's personifications of them are restrained. Not adoring them, he is free to look at them simply for what they are—beautiful and even useful components of the created order.

At the same time, Sirach does not regard the heavenly bodies as having a "separate existence," so to speak. He looks at them solely in their relationship to God and man. He strives for no objective, detached, scientific perspective on them. He treats them, rather, as he would treat household pets: creatures of God that are useful and delightful to men.

From the stars and heavenly bodies Sirach next moves to the phenomena of the atmosphere. He begins with the rainbow (vv. 11–12). We recall that the rainbow, which was not mentioned among the works accomplished by God during the six days of Creation, first appears in Holy Scripture as the sign of the covenant with Noah in Genesis 9. In the present chapter, where Sirach considers nature and not history, he does not mention the rainbow's place in that primeval covenant. Here he speaks only of the rainbow's intense beauty and great majesty, expressing God's (literal!) *arch*itecture: "It circles heaven with its glorious *arc*."

In this treatment of the rainbow, therefore, Sirach lays an emphasis quite different from that of Genesis, which treats of it solely within the Noachic covenant and says nothing about the rainbow's beauty. It is worth observing that when Sirach writes of that covenant in the next chapter (44:18), he says nothing about the rainbow.

From the rainbow he turns his attention to other phenomena of the atmosphere, starting with the snow and lightning (v. 13). This parallel is an example of contrast: the snow falls slowly, the lightning with speed (*tachynei*). In forming this contrast, Sirach is simply applying an observation made in the previous chapter: "All things are in pairs, one opposite the other" (42:24).

As for ourselves, we are not likely to juxtapose snow and lightning, since in nature they rarely appear together. Sirach, however, is looking beyond these phenomena to their Maker, because both the snow and the lightning fall at His "command." In all such physical phenomena Sirach points to the activity of God; all these things happen "by His will" (*en thelemati Avtou*, v. 16).

Continuing this pattern of juxtaposed opposites, our author next joins the softness of the clouds with the hardness of the hailstones (vv. 14–15), and the stability of the mountains with the fluidity of the winds (v. 16).

These are examples of a literary technique supported by the couplet style characteristic of biblical poetry—its sustained preference for binary and parallel constructions. One of the ways of employing this preference is by the insertion of contrasts, the method Sirach uses in these verses.

Another way of using binary and parallel construction, however, is by the insertion of components that do, in fact, commonly go together, whether in nature or by analogy. We are familiar with this style from Psalm 148 and Daniel's canticle of the three young men in the furnace.

This is the method Sirach adopts in the verses that follow, combining things that normally go together, whether in nature or by common associations: thunder and wind (v. 17), snow and frost (vv. 18–19), freezing wind and icy water (v. 20), hot winds and scorched vegetation (v. 21), mist and a sense of refreshment (v. 22).

Sirach next turns his attention to the sea, with the constant agitation of the water, moving around the stable islands (v. 23). It is in this context that he introduces man, who travels far on those seas and returns to recount his amazing stories.

Curiously, it is with the sea that Sirach introduces the phenomenon of narrative, because stories take their rise in adventures (vv. 25–26).

And this, it seems, marks Sirach's approach to creation as a whole: It provides the stuff of adventure, if the beholder gazes upon it with the eye of gratitude. The gratitude will spawn a sense of wonder, because all these things come to us from a loving and provident God.

A selfish person, however, unable to be grateful, will insist on regarding the created works of God only as natural occurrences. Thus, they become only the occasions of boredom and ennui.

Sirach finishes this chapter by a reflection on the transcendence of God (vv. 27–33). The sum of all that can be said of God is *to pan estin Avtos*—literally, "The whole is He" (v. 27). Were this assertion to be made outside of a biblical context, it might bear a *pan*-theistic (*to pan*) sense. Perhaps it was to avoid such an impression that Sirach immediately contrasted God with His creatures: *Avtos gar ho megas para panta ta erga Avtou*—"For He is greater than all His works" (v. 28).

It is the biblical doctrine of Creation that encourages the mind to ascend to God from the consideration of His works: *panta gar epoiesen ho Kyrios*—"For the Lord made all things" (v. 33).

The biblical doctrine of Creation "from nothingness" (*ex nihilo*), a teaching unknown to the history of philosophy apart from the Bible, took metaphysics in a new direction, because it removed God from the realm of category. It cut off any notion of an epistemic *continuum*, a noetic continuity between God and anything else. The divine transcendence is absolute. All that joins creatures to the Creator is His creating act—known only in the act of faith—by which all things are held in being.

It is important to emphasize that Creation is a divine mystery, known only as revealed in Holy Scripture—an article of the Creed grasped solely in the theological gift of faith. It is wisdom revealed to the devout: *tois evsebesin edoken Sophian* (v. 33).

Sirach regards the divine transcendence, moreover, as more than intellectual. It is not simply a noetic ecstasy, but a quality of worship and praise. As such it is expressed in exaltation (*hypsountes*, v. 30), magnification (*megalynei*, v. 31), and praise (*doxsazontes*, vv. 28, 30).

Just as the divine transcendence surpasses man's knowledge, so the divine praise surpasses man's strength. Sirach mentions this several times: "as much as you are able," he says, ". . . put forth all your strength; / Do not grow weary" (v. 30). Indeed, "How shall we ever be able to adequately praise Him" (v. 28).

Thus, Sirach does not describe man's worship as quietly contemplative. On the contrary, he speaks of it as laborious and exacting of one's strength. He describes the praise of God in terms of human inadequacy.

Such worship is not presented as "fulfilling." On the contrary, there is much to suggest that it may be frustrating. To praise God, in the way Sirach describes, is to experience our own limitations. It is no wonder that St. Benedict speaks of prayer as "the *work* of God," *opus Dei.*

EXCURSUS:
Sirach and the Wisdom of Solomon

The two latest sapiential books of the Old Testament, the Wisdom of Solomon and the Wisdom of Sirach, have this as their shared and distinguishing characteristic: They both draw attention to the manifestation of divine wisdom in the course and events of history. This approach to wisdom may be contrasted with Holy Scripture's earlier Wisdom traditions, embodied in Proverbs, and the two "problem" books: Job and Ecclesiastes.

In Proverbs the reader sees little concern for history. On the contrary, this book emphasizes the perennial, the timeless and unchanging quality of wisdom, handed down in a practical way from one generation to the next.

In the two "problem" books, Job and Ecclesiastes, the approach to wisdom is likewise non-historical. One can hardly think of any assertion less sensitive to history than that repeated by Ecclesiastes, "There is nothing new under the sun." Job, too, studies the problem of suffering without appealing to any examples beyond that of Job.

While this perennial and timeless aspect of wisdom is certainly not absent from the Wisdom

---

of Solomon and the Wisdom of Sirach, these latter books also display a strong historical interest: They both study Israel's salvation history as the medium through which God manifested His wisdom. Because wisdom is revealed in history, for both these authors the study of history becomes a path to the acquisition of wisdom. This approach is new and fresh in the Bible's Wisdom literature.

Between the Wisdom of Solomon and the Wisdom of Sirach, however, there is also a difference. In the former work the revelation of divine wisdom is conveyed in God's great redemptive deeds, chiefly the Exodus and the giving of the Torah. In Sirach, on the other hand, the divine wisdom is manifest in the lives of Israel's great leaders over the centuries, the "honored men and our fathers," the "famous men" (KJV), whom Sirach proceeds to praise in chapter 44. The praise of these men will take us nearly to the end of this book.

Sirach's purpose in this lengthy section is partly apologetic: he offers the heroes of Israel's history to counter the heroes of Greek and Roman history. In doing this, our author ironically assumes a place in the history of biography. He stands among those writers who appealed to the lives of the ancients as a source of moral instruction. In this respect, Sirach becomes Israel's equivalent of Plutarch, the Greek historian who wrote the *Lives* of the Greeks and Romans as a source book of ethical instruction.

❧ SIRACH 44 ❧

First in this chapter comes an introduction (vv. 1–15), in which Sirach classifies these illustrious ancients by their particular contributions. Thus, he writes of those who governed wisely (v. 2), prophets and teachers (vv. 2–3), musicians and poets (v. 5), men of commerce and social stability (vv. 6–8).

According to Sirach, however, even more great men—alike benefactors and beneficiaries of Israel's history—remain largely obscure, known chiefly to the grateful families they left behind (vv. 9–15). And, what is more important, they are known to God (v. 10).

Sirach's first individual example of the "famous men" is Enoch (v. 16), who is listed second among the heroes of faith in the Epistle to the Hebrews (11:5–6). The Epistle of Jude describes him simply as "the seventh from Adam" (Jude 14). Genesis, after giving Enoch's age as 365 years, says simply, "Enoch walked with God; and he was not, for God took him" (5:24).

Sirach's second hero of old is Noah, described as "perfect and righteous" (v. 17). This description, *teleios dikaios*, is based on the Septuagint text of Genesis 6:9.

Since the author of the Epistle to the Hebrews reserves the adjective "perfect" (*teleios*) exclusively for the Christian dispensation, he does not use it to describe Noah. He does, however, speak of Noah in terms of "righteousness": "By faith Noah, being divinely warned of things not yet seen, moved with godly fear, prepared an ark for the saving of his household, by which he condemned the world and became heir of the righteousness [*dikaiosyne*] which is according to faith" (11:7). St. Peter goes even further, speaking of Noah as "a preacher of righteousness [*dikaiosyne*]" (2 Peter 2:5).

Sirach had just before referred to "covenants" with which these "honored men" were blessed (v. 12). Now he goes on to speak of the "everlasting covenants" that God made with Noah, His pledge never again to destroy all flesh by a flood (v. 18). The use of the plural, "covenants," in this verse may refer simply to the several repetitions of God's covenant oath in Genesis 9. The story of Noah is

Holy Scripture's first mention of a covenant (Genesis 6:18; 9:9–13, 16, 17).

Sirach will return to the theme of "covenants" many times in his narrative of the "honored men" (vv. 20, 22; 45:5, 7, 15, 17, 24, 25; 47:11).

With respect to Abraham's life (vv. 19–21) Sirach draws attention to three points: First, even before the Torah was given through Moses, Abraham already observed it (v. 20). In Genesis the only specific injunction of the Mosaic Law laid on Abraham was that of circumcision; Sirach, however, seems to have something more than this in mind.

Second, there was a divine covenant with Abraham (v. 20). With respect to this point, Sirach draws on both Genesis accounts of the Abrahamic covenant. Thus, from the first account (Genesis 15:5) he takes the promise of a posterity as numerous as the stars (v. 21), augmenting this image with that of the dust of the earth from Genesis 13:16 (cf. 22:17).

Two other components of the Abrahamic covenant Sirach draws from the second account, in Genesis 17. Thus, in his choice of verbs to describe the divine act in the covenant, he prefers to say that God "established [*estesen*] a covenant" (vv. 20, 21). This is the verb (corresponding to the Hebrew *haqim*) used in Genesis 17:7, 19, but not in Genesis 15. Likewise, the injunction of circumcision as a sign of the covenant (v. 20) is found in Genesis 17:10–14, but not in Genesis 15.

Third, Sirach speaks of Abraham's testing (v. 20), referring to the story in Genesis 22. In this trial Abraham "was found faithful" (*hevrethe pistos*; notice that Noah was *hevrethe teleios dikaios* in v. 17).

Sirach's sequence from Noah to Abraham is instructive from the perspective of ecclesiology. Whereas Sirach's treatment of Noah stressed the "remnant" (v. 17), his reflection on Abraham lays an accent on a great expansion; He is described as "a great father of many nations" (v. 19). Both these considerations pertain to biblical ecclesiology; sometimes the people of God appear as a remnant, a select few rescued from the judgments of history, while in other biblical passages they appear as members of God's universal kingdom, embracing all nations, tribes, and tongues.

Both these aspects of ecclesiology are biblical, and each has been manifested during various epochs in the history of salvation. Thus, the Bible describes the company of heaven as composed of every nation, tribe, and tongue, while it also affirms that the narrow gate will admit only a few. In the present text Noah represents a remnant ecclesiology, while the promise to Abraham expresses a universal ecclesiology.

As we move through these first three of Sirach's "honored men," it is possible already to discern a preoccupation determining both his choice of them and the amount of attention he devotes to them. We observe, for instance, that the word "covenant" has appeared three times so far in this chapter (vv. 12, 18, 20). Indeed, Sirach has mentioned the "covenants" quite a number of times prior to the present chapter (11:20; 14:12, 17; 16:22; 17:12; 24:23; 28:7; 38:33; 39:8; 41:19; 42:2).

Sirach's preoccupation with covenants pertains to his view of salvation history. For him Israel is especially the covenanted people, and God's fidelity to these covenants is the force that guides Israel's history. Everything that has transpired in that history is related to Israel's experience of covenant.

Sirach's selection of the Bible's honored men is related to their service of Israel as God's covenanted people. He did not choose these particular men because they were *interesting* in a purely historical or literary sense. He could easily have found more *interesting* characters in Holy Scripture. As we see in his very next example, Sirach devotes only one verse to Jacob, omitting nearly everything a biographer would find *interesting* in this very rich character. Joseph, to whose life and career Genesis devotes a dozen chapters, receives only one verse from Sirach (49:15). The entire Book of Judges, crammed full of fascinating and colorful men, receives exactly two verses from Sirach.

As for the biblical kings, Sirach dismisses them all except David, Solomon, Hezekiah, and Josiah (49:4). Indeed, it is in connection with those kings that he returns to the theme of the remnant (47:22; 48:16). This leaving of a remnant, Sirach believes, can only be explained by God's fidelity to His covenants.

These comments about Sirach's theological preoccupation prepare us for the very brief treatment he gives to Isaac, Jacob, and the

Twelve Patriarchs (vv. 22–23). The lives of these men, which fill thirty chapters in Genesis, receive only two verses in Sirach.

These verses are closely linked to the treatment of Abraham and may be regarded simply as a continuation of that treatment. Thus, when, Sirach says, "with Isaac [God] established the same assurance" (v. 22), we observe that his verb, *estesen*, is identical to that establishing the Abrahamic covenant (v. 20). Indeed, a closer (but necessarily clumsier) translation of verse 22 should read, "He established with Isaac as He had with his father Abraham." This is a clear reference to the Abrahamic covenant, of which he has just spoken.

And this is the sum of Sirach's interest in Isaac: He was the heir of the covenant with Abraham and the recipient of the same blessings. Isaac represents the succeeding "generation" (vv. 1, 16) in which God's care of His people is preserved. Sirach's interest in Isaac has to do entirely with God's fidelity to His covenant and promises. He is a link in salvation history.

This continuity of covenant is likewise manifest in Jacob: "A blessing for all men and the covenant He made / Rest upon the head of Jacob" (v. 23). Indeed, it is in Jacob's multiple offspring—the Twelve Patriarchs—that Sirach sees the divine promise that Abraham would be the father of many children (v. 21). It is with Jacob that biblical interest starts to turn from select persons to an entire nation.

EXCURSUS:
Enoch

The memory of ancient Enoch greatly intrigued the writers of Israel's later Wisdom literature. For example, Enoch caught the attention of the author of the Wisdom of Solomon, who expanded on the account in Genesis. He wrote of Enoch:

There was once a man pleasing [*euarestos*]
    to God and loved by Him,
And while living among sinners he was
    taken up [*metetethe*].
He was caught up lest evil change his
    understanding

Or deceit deceive his soul.
For envy arising from lack of judgment
    obscures what is good,
And a whirling of desire undermines an
    innocent heart.
He was made perfect [*teleotheis*],
For in a short time he fulfilled long years,
For his soul was pleasing [*areste*] to the
    Lord;
Therefore, He took him early from the
    midst of evil. (4:10–14)

It is significant that the author of Hebrews cites this testimony about Enoch from the Wisdom of Solomon: "By faith Enoch was taken away [*metethe*] so that he did not see death, 'and was not found [*ouk eurisketo*], because God had taken [*metetheken*] him'; for before he was taken [*metatheseos*] he had this testimony, that he pleased [*euariestekenai*] God" (11:5).

The testimony to Enoch here in Sirach uses some of the same vocabulary, saying that Enoch was pleasing to God (*euerestesen*) and was removed (*metetethe*). Sirach goes on, however, to root man's historical quest of God in the example of Enoch, calling him a *hypodeigma metanoias tais genais*—"model of conversion for the generations" (my literal translation). Perhaps this foundation of conversion (*metanoia*) is the reason Sirach begins his list of moral men with Enoch.

Such conversion is the beginning of the quest for God. He pleased God—even to the point that God removed him from the earth—by turning completely to God. As Genesis says, "Enoch walked with God." He did what the Lord later commanded Abraham to do: "Be pleasing before Me and blameless" (Genesis 17:1).

Enoch, we recall, was not a Jew. Living earlier than Noah, he was not even part of the covenant with that early patriarch. Indeed, Enoch was undoubtedly a cave man. Anyway, he is our most primitive example of a man who relied entirely on the early religious tradition of the human race. Yet he pleased God. He pleased God so much that God took him up, because the world was not worthy of him.

What did Enoch know of God? According to the Epistle to the Hebrews, he knew only that God "is, and that He is a rewarder of those who diligently seek Him" (11:6). That simple metaphysical and moral truth, however, was quite enough. The very thought of God's existence made all the difference between a worldly man and a godly man.

Enoch, as far as we know, had no other hope. Yet Sirach credits him with being a "model of conversion for the generations," and the Epistle to the Hebrews holds him up to Christians as a champion of the faith. Enoch took very seriously the rather little he knew about God, and he based his life on the little he did know. He made it the foundation of his life.

And what happened? His life was so completely pleasing to God that He took him. God would not be deprived of such a friend. This is the sense in which Enoch has served, almost from the beginning of the human race, as a model of conversion to the nations. Sirach begins, in short, on the principle of conversion—*metanoia*.

EXCURSUS:
Noah and the Remnant

"In a time of wrath," Sirach literally says, Noah "became an *antallagma*" (44:17). The obscurity of this reference likely accounts for the rather imaginative translation in the *Orthodox Study Bible*: "he was rescued in exchange." By way of explaining this translation, a footnote in that same source says, "Noah by his righteous life became a propitiation for the whole human race."

Both this translation and its explanation, however, are very improbable. Sirach uses the word *antallagma* only two other times, neither of them in the context of sacrifice, and both of them in the simple, ordinary sense of "substitute" (6:15; 26:14). Indeed, this is the normal meaning of *antallagma* in the Septuagint (cf. Ruth 4:7; 3 Kingdoms 20:2; Job 28:15; Amos 5:12; Jeremiah 15:13). Hence, this should be the translation of the present text as well: "In the time of wrath, he became a substitute."

In what sense did Noah become a substitute? In the immediate context Noah appears on the earth as a substitute for Enoch, the righteous man who, just one verse earlier, had just been taken away. Indeed, according to the calculations in Genesis 5, Noah was born only 67 years after Enoch disappeared.

Like Genesis, Sirach is listing the righteous men in their "generations" (*tais genais*—44:16). As Enoch had been the "model of conversion" (*hypodeigma metanoias*) to those biblical generations, so Noah became his "substitute" (*antallagma*). That is to say, even in that very sinful time, "a time of wrath," the Lord did not leave the human race without a just man to model the ways of conversion.

This was the reason "a remnant was left on the earth / When the flood came." Much of the continuing narrative in Genesis is about a "remnant" that is left after the Lord goes through a historical process of selection, in which certain men (Ishmael, Esau, and so forth) are rejected in favor of others whom God chooses. Thus, this word "remnant" (*kataleimma*) described the house of Jacob when Joseph saved them from the famine (Genesis 45:7), and Sirach, in the only other place where he uses the word, will cite that text in 47:22.

∾ SIRACH 45 ∾

The present chapter is devoted to three characters, all of them from the tribe of Levi: Moses, Aaron, and Phineas. Between them, Moses and Phineas must share nine verses; the remaining seventeen belong to Aaron, making obvious Sirach's great interest in Israel's worship and priesthood.

The grandeur of Moses, in the eyes of Sirach, came from his privilege of direct access to God to receive the Torah, which was the very embodiment of divine wisdom (vv. 3, 5). The gift of the Torah took place in the context of a special covenant (*diatheke*) on Mount Sinai.

In describing Moses as "a man of mercy" (v. 1), Sirach may have had in mind his intercession to waylay the Lord's resolve to destroy the people in the desert (Exodus 32:11–14).

In describing Moses as "equal in glory to the saints" (v. 2), Sirach probably had in mind the radiance emanating from his countenance by reason of his proximity to the divine glory (Exodus 34:33–35; 2 Corinthians 3:13). This is consonant with Sirach's reminder that God spoke to Moses "face to face" (v. 5).

The Torah, that is to say, is not a work of religious speculation. It is God's very Word, conveyed face-to-face with Moses, providing infallible guidance for human life. It is the sublime embodiment of God's will for man, and therefore—in the mind of Sirach—the most perfect expression of wisdom.

Sirach stresses Moses' relationship to the secular powers represented by Pharaoh (v. 3). This emphasis reflects our author's interest in declaring Israel's competence before the claims of the pagan world. Israel, Sirach intends to declare, needs to quaver before Greek power no more than Moses did before Egyptian power. Indeed, the latter was afraid of Moses (v. 2).

Moses was sanctified for his "faithfulness and gentleness" (v. 4). That is to say, faithfulness and gentleness are the marks of sanctity. The adjective of the noun translated here as "gentleness"—*prayetes*—is used to describe Jesus in the Gospel of Matthew (11:29; 21:5).

The darkness into which Moses was led (v. 5) apparently refers to the cloud that he entered to hear God's words on Mount Sinai. They are symbolic of the depth of his religious experience. Indeed, this religious experience is the chief object of Sirach's interest in Moses. He was an able leader of the people, because he was an intimate of God. The wisdom conveyed in the Torah was the fruit of Moses' experience of God in the cloud on the mountain. What Moses accomplished in the valley of life came directly from the wisdom into which he was initiated on the mountain. His active life flowed from his contemplation of the divine glory.

Aaron receives seventeen verses (6–22) in the Book of Sirach, more than any other of the "honored men" except the high priest Simon II (50:1–21). For Sirach, these two men stood at the extremes of the Aaronic priesthood: the first was the earliest of Israel's high priests, and the other had only recently died (about 195 BC).

Staying with the tribe of Levi, Sirach follows his reflections on the priesthood of Aaron by a consideration of his grandson, Phineas (vv. 23–26). The latter he calls "the third in glory" (*trios eis doxsan*), evidently in sequence to Moses and Aaron. With Phineas, too, "there was established a covenant of peace" (my translation of *estathe diatheke eirenes* in v. 24).

Once again we observe Sirach's preference for the priestly vocabulary of Genesis 9 and 17, where the covenant is described as "established." This preference is consistent with his theology of history, in which worship holds primacy of place.

The zeal (*zelosai*) of Phineas, celebrated in Numbers 25 and Psalm 105 (106), is given as the reason for the Lord's special regard for him. Inspired by a strong sense of God's holiness, Phineas endeavored to see that holiness expressed in Israel's moral life. Perceiving the moral danger inherent in Israel's contamination with the Moabites, Phineas seized the hour; he also seized a spear and made swift work of the danger. Thus, says Sirach, "he made atonement for Israel."

Suddenly, however, somewhat abruptly, and certainly out of sequence, Sirach begins speaking of God's covenant with David (v. 25). Since he will treat David later on in the historical order where we would expect to find him (47:1–11), why does David appear here in the context of the Aaronic priesthood?

The reason, I believe, is related to what appears to be a sustained theme in the post-exilic literature: the theological and historical relationship between kingship and hierarchy in Israel. When Sirach treats the covenant with Israel's royal house in the context of the covenant with Israel's priesthood, he is following a pattern clear in two other post-exilic writers, one a prophet and the other a historian.

The prophet is Zechariah, who describes Israel's royalty and priesthood as the two olive trees that provide oil for Israel's illumination (4:1–7). The historian is the Chronicler, in whose perspective the priestly and royal covenants—the houses of Aaron and David—provide for Israel the twin parts of an integral ministry.

Following this same pattern, when Sirach treats of the priestly covenant exemplified in Aaron and Phineas, he feels compelled, as it were, to speak immediately of the companion covenant with the royal house of David. Like Zechariah and the Chronicler, he avoids dealing with either institution—priesthood or kingship—separately from the other. Thus, the theological and historical relationship between these two institutions is given a post-exilic stress in a Wisdom writer, along with a prophet and a historian.

The author of the Epistle to the Hebrews, writing under the impulse of his Christology, will find both institutions prefigured in Melchizedek (7:1).

The final verse of the present chapter is a benediction on the high priests, Israel's recognized leaders at the time of Sirach. Aware of the spiritual dangers to which some of these high priests have succumbed, Sirach prays for an increase in their wisdom.

EXCURSUS:
Sirach and the Priesthood

There is twofold significance, I believe, in the fact that Sirach devoted his two longest and most detailed reflections to two representatives of the priesthood.

First, there is a polemical background to Sirach's reflections. Since the death of Simon II, the high priesthood had become something of a political prize, so that during the second century some unworthy and unfaithful men, who had purchased that office from Israel's Seleucid overlords, served the temple at Jerusalem.

That is to say, Israel had recently experienced some very bad high priests, whose evil deeds are recorded in the Books of the Maccabees. In that context Sirach was at pains to declare what the office of the priesthood was *supposed* to be.

Second, Sirach's interest in the priesthood pertains to his understanding of Israel's history. Like the Chronicler, to whom he is something of a spiritual heir, Sirach thinks of Israel's history chiefly in terms of her worship. He is among those biblical theologians convinced that the covenanted people was especially defined by its relationship to God in worship.

It is instructive to observe that both Sirach and the Epistle to the Hebrews, in finishing their accounts of biblical history, go on to describe scenes of worship (50:13–21; Hebrews 12:22–24). In both books, biblical history arrives at its culmination in God's people assembled to worship Him. Just as the meaning of all history is to be found in the history of God's people (the great thesis of St. Augustine's *The City of God*), so the history of God's people finds its meaning in God's eternal worship. In this respect, both Sirach and the author of Hebrews seem deeply indebted to the theology of the Chronicler.

With Aaron, says Sirach, God "established an everlasting covenant"—*estesen diatheken ainos* (45:7; cf. *eis diatheken aionos* in 45:15). We observe the same vocabulary used by a priestly hand in Genesis to describe the covenants with Noah (9:9, 11, 16) and Abraham (17:7).

Sirach meditates on the symbolism of the sacred vestments worn by the high priest, a subject to which he will return when he describes the ministry of Simon II. The priest is properly adorned in ritual garb to beautify the people's worship, and for more than three thousand years the people of God have found all manner of symbolism in the priestly vestments. For example, Sirach continues Israel's understanding of the twelve stones on the breastplate of the high priest as symbolizing the twelve tribes, the fullness of the people of God (45:11).

In addition to the offering of the regular and daily sacrifices (45:14–16), the sons of Aaron are also to be teachers of the people, instructors in the meaning of the Torah. This teaching ministry of the priesthood, which perhaps began during the Babylonian Exile of the sixth century, is very important to Sirach (45:17). Since that time to the present, the ministry of the priest has included the responsibility of instructing God's people.

~: SIRACH 46 :~

From his consideration of priests, Sirach turns next to the warriors. Indeed, he found a natural point of this transition in the character of Phineas, the priest that wielded the spear (45:23–24).

That zealous priest, followed by the warriors—Joshua, Caleb, and the judges—had a particular relevance to the time when Sirach was writing. It was an era in which the claims of God were chiefly vindicated by a priestly family of warriors—the Maccabees. These latter, along with the zealous Jews who joined them, could draw strength from the examples of Joshua, Caleb, and the judges, who waged war in ancient times against the enemies of God's people.

From all the stories about Joshua, Sirach especially concentrates on those pertinent to warfare—specifically, for control of the Holy Land (vv. 1–6). These stories, he perceived, were more relevant to recent times, when the successors of Alexander the Great vied with one another for control over the Holy Land.

Sirach's description of Joshua includes the etymology of his name (v. 1), which means "the Lord saves." We recognize here the given name of Christ our Savior. As the instrument of the Lord's salvation, Joshua led the conquest of the cities of Palestine (v. 2), beginning with Jericho.

Like the pagans afflicting the Jews of Sirach's time, those ancient Canaanites were idolaters who resisted Israel's God, and among the descriptions of the Lord, Joshua especially knew Him as the Lord of armies. Hence, the battles fought by Joshua were "the wars for the Lord" (v. 3).

The Lord's warrior fought not only with the sword but also with prayer, and Sirach recalls how the day was lengthened through Joshua's intercession (v. 4; Joshua 10:12–14). Essential to the victories of Joshua was the fact that "He called upon the Most High," and "the great Lord answered him" (v. 5).

To Joshua, Sirach adds the name of his famous companion, Caleb, remembering that those two men had urged Israel to conquer the Holy Land in the time of Moses (vv. 7–8). To Sirach's contemporaries—many of them tempted to an apostate defection to Hellenism—the example of these two historical characters served as a salutary admonition. Just as the great mass of Israelites had succumbed to idolatry and refused to enter the Holy Land at the time of Moses, so too were many of Sirach's contemporaries bewitched by the religion and culture of Hellenism. Such men were to be resisted, as Joshua and Caleb had held fast in the desert.

To these two champions of faith, Sirach joins the heroes in the Book of Judges, though he does not name any of them in particular.

We trace, thus, the development of Sirach's theme. He began with those heroes associated with the ancient covenants that created God's people (44:16–23). From there he went to Israel at worship (45:1–26). In the present chapter he moves to Israel at war (vv. 1–12). Indeed, Sirach sees no discrepancy in this development from worship to warfare, because Israel's religion is the root of the warfare. Because the Lord is one, the gods of the nations must be resisted. It is their worship that causes God's people to wage war.

The final figure in this chapter (vv. 13–20), Samuel, succeeds to both the worship and the warfare that Sirach regards as inseparable.

Samuel is treated in Holy Scripture very much as a transitional figure. Even though regarded as the last of the judges, he does not appear in the Book of Judges. Indeed, most of what we know about Samuel is found in connection with Israel's first two kings, both of whom he anointed.

This literary perspective is very much in line with history itself. Samuel rightly has a place in Sirach's list because he did, in fact, span an extremely difficult period in Israel's history—he was a man of transition.

The last of the judges, Samuel was not a judge in the sense of a charismatic warrior, like several of the others. Nonetheless, a charismatic warrior—a replacement for Samson, as it were—was what Israel needed during that time after the Philistines invaded.

In asking for a king, in fact, what the Israelites initially wanted was someone to lead them into battle (1 Kingdoms 8:20), and Israel's first king, Saul, was very much the warrior. Samuel himself was more of a spiritual leader, and in this capacity he continued to minister after the monarchy was established.

The biblical chapters devoted to Samuel's ministry testify that he lived during a time of great turmoil and disturbance. Because of Babylon's decline on the east side of the Fertile Crescent in the late eleventh century, along with the weakness of Egypt's twenty-first dynasty on the west side, the whole region experienced constant tribal and small-scale warfare and political upheaval, such as we see in the Book of Judges. The low spiritual tone and lack of spiritual discernment are indicated in the final verse of that book: "Each man did what was proper in his own eyes" (21:25, my translation of the Codex Alexandrinus).

This verse says a great deal about the task to which Samuel devoted his entire life. During this time of profound transition, when the people were morally floundering, he was a man of prayer (v. 16) and insight (v. 15), called to speak for God and to discern God's will for Israel. In so doing he was arguably less the heir of the judges than the successor of Moses. Samuel supremely exemplified the social responsibilities of the wise man, a theme that appears so prominently in the Books of 1 & 2 Kingdoms. Never a king, Samuel—more ably, I think, than Solomon—best illustrated the ideals of Plato's philosopher-king.

It is not surprising that Sirach identifies Samuel first as a prophet (v. 13; cf. v. 15). Even as a young man, he was universally recognized as a prophet (1 Kingdoms 28:14–20). Even death, in fact, did not stop him from his prophetic ministry, says Sirach (v. 20), obviously referring to Saul's séance with the witch of Endor (1 Kingdoms 28:14–20). This portrayal of Samuel as a prophet continues in the New Testament, where he is so identified in all three places where he is mentioned (Acts 3:24; 13:20; Hebrews 11:32).

Even though Samuel initially opposed the establishing of a monarchy, Sirach recognizes his influence in the founding of that kingdom (*katestesen basileian*) which would, in due course, replace Israel's traditional tribal leadership.

Samuel, particularly in his confrontations with King Saul, set up the prophetic standard for later prophets who were obliged to speak sternly to kings: Nathan to David, Hanani to Asa, Michaiah and Elijah to Ahab, Isaiah to Ahaz, Jeremiah to Zedekiah, Daniel to Belshazzar, and John the Baptist to Herod.

EXCURSUS:
Sirach and Ibn al-Arabi

In his lengthy moral analysis of Israel's honored men, Sirach examined them as types. In fact, he began that treatment by listing them according to type (44:3–15).

None of these biblical heroes, however, was simply *reduced* to a type. Each was permitted to be himself, because Sirach was interested in them as distinct persons within specific historical contexts. Their immortality, guaranteed by the Bible (including Sirach's own book), did not render them timeless.

In this respect it will be instructive to contrast Sirach's treatment of these ancient men with an approach to the prophets that is common in Islam. In Islamic theology the biblical prophets are largely separated from their context in biblical history. I do not mean that the Qu'ran denies the historicity of their revelation. It is more the case that the historical settings of the prophets are largely ignored; those historical settings do not serve as the context for understanding prophetic teaching.

According to Qu'ranic thought, each of the prophets was given to grasp some segment or aspect of the total and unified message of Islam. Those prophets—a group that includes several non-biblical religious men known to the Arabs—were charged with speaking limited parts of the fullness of revelation given finally in the Qu'ran itself. In a manner sharply in contrast to Sirach, the prophetic message in the Qu'ran is unified, not by reference to the unity of Israel's history—and certainly not by reference to its fulfillment in Christ—but through the plenary revelation granted through Muhammad.

Understood in this way, each of the prophets represents some aspect of man's approach to God. They were religious "types." Indeed, certain scholars of the Qu'ran, some of them taking their lead from Plato, elaborated typologies of the prophetic thought and experience.

Arguably the best of these efforts was that of Ibn al-Arabi (1165–1240), who elaborated his theory of the prophets in *The Bezels of Wisdom*. This author, whom his contemporaries surnamed *Ibn Aflatun* ("Son of Plato"), wrote on the theme of wisdom in twenty-seven of the prophets mentioned in the Qu'ran, most of them biblical. In these *bezels*, or "seals," he discovered some special aspect of wisdom manifested in each of these prophets. Thus, he meditated on the wisdom of destiny in Ezra, the wisdom of intimacy in Elijah, the wisdom of holiness in Enoch, and so forth. According to Ibn al-Arabi, the one wisdom was revealed to each of these prophets according to his particular ability to receive it.

The merits of this engaging theory are obvious. When Ibn al-Arabi wrote the *Bezels* toward the end of his life, it was arguably the best and most attractive Platonic reading of the biblical material since Philo a millennium earlier.

I cannot help but wonder, nonetheless, what Isaiah might say on finding his message wrenched from its historical context and subsumed into a large panorama of eternal and universal religious truth. In fact, Isaiah need not worry, because he is not found in the *Bezels*; Ibn al-Arabi mentioned neither him nor most of Israel's other "literary" prophets. The reason for this omission is simple: Ibn al-Arabi was not really interested in the teaching of the prophets. Very unlike Sirach, he used them, rather, only as symbols of his own religious teaching.

This work of Ibn al-Arabi is justly revered among proponents of the Perennial Philosophy—those persuaded that man's ongoing search for God is essentially identical at all times, though manifest differently in different historical and cultural settings.

This Islamic approach to the prophets, however, is almost infinitely distant from that of Sirach, and of the Bible generally. In our Holy Scriptures, the prophets and holy men—the honored men of Israel—are neither religious theorists nor partial symbols of eternal truth. They are essentially men who addressed the circumstances of their own times, convinced that God was revealing Himself in the fabric of those times. The unity among the prophets is founded on the unity of that history.

EXCURSUS:
Dividing Biblical History

A common way of dividing Old Testament history is based on the era of the monarchy. For example, Matthew traced the genealogy of Jesus according to three distinct periods: pre-monarchical (1:2–6), monarchical (1:7–11), and post-monarchical (1:12–16). Thus, wrote Matthew, there were "all the generations from Abraham to David . . . from David to the captivity in Babylon . . . and from the captivity in Babylon to the Christ" (1:17).

Needless to say, the division of history by recourse to political periods is a common pattern of historiography. Historians of Rome, for instance, have always parceled the material by reference to the Republic and the Empire, and the emperors themselves serve as signposts to identify the various periods of the Empire.

When we come to biblical history, however, this kind of division presents a methodological difficulty, for the simple reason that Israel's political history is less significant than other theological concerns. The Bible is more about God's activity than man's.

This narrative difficulty was perceived already in the second century before Christ, I believe, for we detect it here in Sirach's survey of Israel's "famous men." When he came to the transition from the age of the judges to the monarchy, Sirach was faced with a bit of a problem: How to get from Samuel to David without having to deal with Saul? He certainly could not include Saul among his "famous men"!

Sirach got around this problem by resorting to a curious maneuver: Instead of tracing the continuous history from the judges to the monarchy, he tracked it through the prophetic ministry: He angled over from Samuel to the Bible's next prophet—Nathan.

That step from Samuel to Nathan was perfectly consistent and provided a seamless robe of narrative, in which Sirach could tie together two periods of Israel's political history—the judges and the monarchy—without the category of politics. Moving from Samuel to Nathan (47:1) permitted Sirach to sidestep deftly from the judges to Israel's second king: David. Having omitted Saul altogether, he then proceeded to consign most of the other kings (Solomon excepted, of whom he was critical) to the realm of silence.

Thus, Sirach concentrated on the prophets—not the kings—during the period of the monarchy. The two kings he felt obliged to include—Hezekiah and Josiah—were combined with two prophets with whom they were contemporary, Isaiah (48:17–25) and Jeremiah (49:1–7) respectively.

It is not difficult to see why Sirach approached the matter this way. Most of the biblical kings hardly merited inclusion among his "famous men," whereas the biblical prophets most certainly did. He was not writing a history of Israel but a sequential account of Israel's "famous men."

Without referring to Sirach on the point, Saint Augustine also believed Israel's monarchical period was really more about the prophets than the kings. That whole era (*hoc itaque tempus*), he wrote, from Samuel down through the Babylonian Captivity, was "the age of the prophets"—*totum tempus est prophetarum.* Other men, to be sure, "both before and after" that period, are called prophets, but the years between Samuel and the Babylonian Captivity "are especially and chiefly called the days of the prophets"—*dies prophetarum praecipue maximeque hi dicti sunt* (*The City of God* 17.1).

In our translated Bibles, we tend still to divide the material by way of reference to Israel's political systems: We move from the era of the judges to the establishment of the monarchy in 1 & 2 Kingdoms, and then to the history of the monarchy in 3 & 4 Kingdoms. In the Hebrew Bible, on the other hand, all the books from Joshua through Malachi— covering nearly a thousand years—are under one category: "The Prophets," or *Nebivim.*

We detect that earlier perspective also in passing references within the New Testament. Thus, the Epistle to the Hebrews mentioned "Samuel and the prophets" to designate the biblical history after David (11:32). St. Peter, too, spoke of "all the prophets, from Samuel and those who follow" (Acts 3:24).

❦ SIRACH 47 ❦

There are three points to be made about Sirach's treatment of David (vv. 1–11):

First, like Israel's earlier historians, the authors of 1 & 2 Kingdoms, Sirach stresses David's military exploits, beginning with the slaying of Goliath (vv. 4–5). In connection with these exploits he speaks of David's physical strength and courage, saying that he sported (*epaichsen*) with lions and bears (v. 3). David went on, Sirach records, to destroy the enemies that surrounded Israel, especially the Philistines. The king so thoroughly trounced the latter that they could never again pose a military threat to God's people (vv. 6–7).

In the verses Sirach devotes to the stories by Israel's earlier historians, we gain a new perspective about the meaning of wisdom: Wisdom can be expressed in military strength and physical courage, when these replace the service of God and His people. As a warrior, David inherited the mantle of Joshua, the character with whom Sirach began the previous chapter (46:1–6). Like Joshua, David made prayer a component of his combat, which was thereby strengthened beyond merely human measure.

Second, this mention of prayer introduces a feature of David that Sirach draws mainly from the Chronicler, one of Israel's later historians. Like the Chronicler, Sirach emphasizes David's important role in the history of Israel's worship, especially his provision for the sacred music (vv. 8–9) and the observance of festivals (v. 10). Unlike David's military exploits, this fruit of his liturgical work was still obvious in Sirach's day.

Third, Sirach's comments on David were particularly pertinent to his contemporaries in the second century before Christ. This pertinence seems especially clear in David's sins and repentance. Whereas the Chronicler had made no reference to David's famous sins, Sirach apparently considered them important to a complete picture of Israel's second king. Thus, he begins his treatment of David by a reference to Nathan, whose prophetic message led the king to repentance. It is with this repentance—and the subsequent covenant, also announced by Nathan—that he closes his treatment of David. In beginning and ending the story of David with the theme of repentance, Sirach was calling his unfaithful contemporaries to a heartfelt conversion. The only sin that definitively impedes the attaining of wisdom is unrepented sin.

Consequently, in summoning the lessons of Israel's history for the moral and spiritual benefit of his own countrymen, Sirach directed their notice to David as a repentant and forgiven sinner.

Sirach, when he came to the successors of David (vv. 12–25), must have felt a certain measure of embarrassment, requiring an adjustment in the thread of his narrative. We already considered how gingerly he sidestepped the period of the judges, barely mentioning them in a general way (46:11–12) before going on to concentrate on Samuel (46:13–20). Although the period of the monarchy was scarcely more edifying than that of the judges, Sirach was unable to use the same approach to the monarchy, and this for two reasons.

First, it was too long a period in Israel's history, lasting from Solomon's accession to the throne in 961 BC until the Babylonian destruction of Jerusalem in 587. It was the monarchy that gave institutional coherence to those nearly four centuries. Although Israel's historians—the authors of Kingdoms and Chronicles—recorded very little evidence of royal wisdom during that long period, Sirach could not bypass this one institution that provided narrative continuity to Israel's history. His list of "famous men," after all, did not embrace a list of individuals; it was, rather, the evidence of wisdom's persistent presence throughout Israel's history.

Second, Sirach was faced with the painful irony that the rare and spotty virtue manifest in the history of Israel's monarchy began with the king most reputed for wisdom—Solomon! Because of his legendary reputation for wisdom, it was necessary to include Solomon among the "famous men," even though the inclusion would have to be seriously qualified.

Sirach handled this delicate problem of historiography with a careful analysis of Solomon. Indeed, he is more critical of Solomon than of any other of his "famous men." Solomon, Sirach suggests, was able to think and act wisely, because his father had bequeathed to him the political stability and security requisite to leisure and the habit of reflection: David had placed Solomon "in a broad space," *en platysmo* (v. 12). The peace of Solomon's early reign made possible the completion of his most important effort, the construction of the temple (v. 13). This temple embodied divine wisdom.

Pursuing the apologetic intent never far from his mind, Sirach stresses that the other nations were instructed by Solomon's insights and counsels during that early period (vv. 14–17). Truly, Israel's vocation to teach wisdom to the other nations was arguably best exemplified in the case of Solomon.

Nonetheless, Solomon's fall from grace also best illustrated the dangers that accompany political success and financial prosperity, and this, too, demonstrated a point of irony: Solomon's political success and financial prosperity were the fruit of his wise government (v. 18); he, above all men in Holy Scripture, exemplified Plato's ideal of the philosopher-king.

Yet, this success and prosperity also precipitated Solomon's downfall. He showed himself to be the sort of man mourned by the Psalmist: "A man being in honor did not understand; / He was compared to the senseless cattle, and became like them" (Psalm 48[49]:13).

A powerful and prosperous king, Solomon in due course resurrected the arrogance of Saul, losing all sense of proportion and discipline. This loss was expressed in his conquest of women. Sirach, unlike the authors of Kingdoms and Chronicles, does not trace Solomon's historical downfall to the idolatry these women introduced into Israel. He traces it, rather, to physical lust as an expression of spiritual arrogance. Solomon possessed women as a man might possess any other luxury in life. He was weakened through his body (*enexsousiasthes en to somatic sou*, v. 19). Quite simply, Solomon was morally reduced by his lust, which was less a perversion of sex than an abuse of power.

The first result of this reduction, moreover, was the division of the kingdom that followed directly on his death. Solomon's loss of "good sense" (*katanygenai epi te aphronsyne sou*, v. 20) was passed on to his sons, starting with Rehoboam (v. 23).

De facto, then, Solomon had two political successors, Rehoboam in the south and Jeroboam in the north, both of them fools (vv. 23–25). These are the only foolish individuals listed among the "famous men."

For all that, nonetheless, "the Lord did not abandon His mercy / Nor corrupt any of His words" (v. 22). For this reason, Sirach's narrative of wisdom goes on, his concentration shifting to the prophets of the monarchical period.

Having mentioned Jeroboam I at the end of the previous chapter (47:24), Sirach accordingly turns his attention northward, to consider Elijah and Elisha, the two prophets sent by the Lord to the schismatic kingdom of Samaria (vv. 1–16). In treating of these ninth-century prophets, Sirach pursues an interest not much shared by the Chronicler, who largely ignored these men (and the rest of northern history).

First came Elijah (vv. 1–11), whose prophetic vocation inspired so many pages of the Books of Kingdoms. Sirach likens this energetic figure to a fire (v. 1), a comparison justified by Elijah's style, not least on those occasions when he summoned fire down from heaven (v. 3). This image of fire returns in the scene of the prophet's dramatic departure from this world (v. 9).

Taking up an emphasis common throughout his reflections, Sirach regards Elijah in terms of the wise man's duties to society. Although this prophet was something of a recluse (cf. 3 Kingdoms 17:2–4; 18:10), Sirach stresses Elijah's ministry in Israel's public and political life: his challenges to the corrupt royal house (v. 6), his anointings of kings and prophets (v. 8), and his ministry to the little family at Zarephath (v. 5).

Elijah's leave-taking from this world was as intense as the other events in his life (v. 9). Since he did not die, moreover, this prophet was expected to return to earth in the future, in order to "calm the wrath of God before it breaks forth in fury, / To turn the heart of the father to the son, / And to restore the tribes of Jacob" (v. 10). In this assertion of hope, we recognize Sirach's debt to the prophet Malachi (3:22 [in the Hebrew text, 4:5–6]; cf. Luke 1:17).

In the course of our meditations on Sirach, we have often had occasion to remark on wisdom's relation to history, a strong theme in this book. We see in his treatment of Elijah an extension of this theme to eschatology—to the goal of history. This goal he calls "the proper time," literally "unto times" (*eis kairous*, v. 10). The prophets were the great unifiers of Israel's experiences, gathering into a synthesis the sundry times and events of history, relating widely distant events to one another by way of historical interpretation, guiding the conscience to the understanding of God's purpose, and finally directing the movement of history toward its fulfillment. Sirach follows the insight of Malachi by indicating the role of Elijah in that work of prophecy.

The prophet Elisha, the chief figure in the few remaining verses Sirach devoted to the Northern Kingdom (vv. 12–16), is mainly remembered as a thaumaturge, a worker of wonders, not only during his lifetime, but even after his death. This last detail Sirach found in the incident recorded in 4 Kingdoms 13:21, which speaks of a dead man who was revived as his body came into contact with the bones of Elisha.

According to Sirach, that event was not only a miracle (*terata . . . thavmasia ta erga*, v. 14), but also a prophecy. Indeed, Elisha's "body prophesied" (*eprophetevsen to soma*, v. 13). Such a prophecy, mentioned immediately before Israel's destruction by Assyria in 722 BC (v. 15), was important to Sirach, because it pointed to the coming restoration of the Chosen People.

Sirach recognizes that deeds, as well as works, can bear prophetic meaning. St. Augustine speaks of a *prophetia facti etiam ipsa, non verbi, id scilicet facto significans*—"itself a prophecy of deed, not of word, actually signifying by a deed" (*The City of God* 17.5).

Speaking of the downfall and dispersion of the Northern Kingdom in 722 (v. 16), Sirach advances his account to the latter part of the eighth century, when the faithful remnant of that kingdom, a "people few in number," welcomed the invitation of King Hezekiah, "a ruler in the house of David," to rejoin the covenanted kingdom of Judah. This happened after Hezekiah's assumption of that throne in 715 (2 Chronicles 30:1–12).

Sirach thus arrives at his next two famous men: Hezekiah the king and Isaiah the prophet (vv. 17–25), contemporary servants of God whose complementary ministries lasted into the second decade of the seventh century.

Sirach begins with Hezekiah's revolt against Assyria, in preparation for which he fortified his capital at Jerusalem and dug an underground aquaduct to provide it with water during times of siege (v. 17). These preparations enabled the city to survive during

Sennacherib's invasion in 701 (vv. 18–20; 4 Kingdoms 18:13—19:37; 2 Chronicles 32:1–23).

This example from history, Sirach believed, provided for his contemporaries an important lesson with respect to God's pagan enemies. Implicit in his account of it is Sirach's conviction that the people of God should not be impressed by the apparently greater resources of the heathen, whether in Hezekiah's time or six hundred years later.

Hezekiah's stay and inspiration during that Assyrian crisis was Isaiah, to whom Sirach devotes the remaining verses of this chapter (vv. 20–25). Isaiah, says Sirach, "saw the last things"—*eiden ta eschata* (v. 24). That is to say, the message of Isaiah was directed to the future, "what was to come to the end of time, / . . . the hidden things" (*ta apokrypha*, v. 25). Like Elijah (v. 10) and Elisha (v. 13), Isaiah spoke for the future of God's people.

Sirach's perspective on Isaiah came to be that of Matthew and the other New Testament writers, who continually cite the testimony of Isaiah as fulfilled in the person, life, and ministry of Jesus.

EXCURSUS:
Those Dry Bones

In the light of Sirach's comment on it, that story of Elisha's death and the dead man's revival deserves a second look. The original account says that on touching the bones of Elisha, the dead man "lived and rose on his feet" (my literal translation of *ezesen kai aneste epi tous podas avtou* in the LXX text of 4 Kingdoms 13:21). This description is almost verbatim what the prophet Ezekiel portrayed in his famous vision of the dry bones: "they lived and stood on their feet" (*ezesan kai estesan epi ton podon avton*, Ezekiel 37:10).

In Ezekiel's original context this resurrection of Israel's slain was a prophecy of the people's restoration after the Babylonian Captivity. In its larger canonical context, it also prophesied God's victory over death in the Resurrection of Christ, "the first fruits of those who have fallen asleep" (1 Corinthians 15:20).

Sirach, perhaps reading the story of the risen dead man through the prophecy of Ezekiel, regarded that miracle as a foretelling of what lay ahead for the people of God. In the next chapter, in fact, where Sirach does treat of Ezekiel (49:9), the reference is followed immediately by the wish that the bones of the twelve minor prophets should be revivified. We will look at that text in its proper sequence.

This interpretation of Sirach is consistent with his earlier mention of the future life of those who fall asleep in love (v. 11). It is also consonant with his treatment of Isaiah near the end of chapter 48, where he speaks of "what was to come to the end of time" (48:25). This keen interest in the fulfillment of prophecy is one of the features that distinguish Sirach from Israel's earlier Wisdom literature. This interest pertains to his theology of history.

EXCURSUS:
Hezekiah

A king praised by Sirach, Hezekiah (715–687 BC) was a young man—only twenty-five—when he assumed the throne of Judah (4 Kingdoms 18:2), because of the relatively short life of his hapless father Ahaz.

The new king, moreover, inherited a mess. His kingdom was impoverished by his father's irresponsibility, and much of the Holy Land lay in ruins from local wars and a recent invasion from afar. Seven years earlier, in 722, the Assyrians had destroyed the kingdom of Israel, to Judah's north, and then deported the great masses of its people to regions over in the far end of the Fertile Crescent.

Furthermore, Hezekiah well knew that his own father had been the culprit responsible for earlier inviting the Assyrians to interfere in the politics of the Holy Land (2 Chronicles 28:16–21). The problem was part of his father's own legacy, then, and the new king himself was obliged to pay annual tribute to Assyria, further impoverishing his realm.

Over the next two decades, however, Hezekiah undertook measures toward resisting that ever-looming menace from the east. First, he endeavored to reunite the remnant of Israelites in the north with his own throne in Jerusalem, thus enlarging his realm by restoring the borders of David's ancient kingdom. In this effort he was somewhat successful (30:1–11).

Second, Hezekiah strengthened Jerusalem's defenses by cutting an underground conduit through solid rock, so that water could be brought secretly into the city from the Gihon Spring. This remarkable feat of technology, unearthed by modern archeology, is recorded not only twice in the Bible (4 Kingdoms 20:20; 2 Chronicles 32:30) but also in the contemporary Siloam Inscription. In this effort Hezekiah was very successful.

Prior to either of these efforts, however, Hezekiah initiated a religious reform, convinced that the nation's recent apostasy under his father Ahaz was the root of Judah's unfortunate plight. Thus, he began his reign by purifying the temple, lately defiled by pagan worship (2 Chronicles 29:3–19), in order to restore the edifice to the proper service of God (29:20–36).

Unlike the unbelieving Ahaz, who treated a spiritual dilemma as merely a political problem, to be addressed by political means, Hezekiah was determined to regard the spiritual dilemma as exactly what it was. Indeed, Hezekiah's programmatic reform maintained the proper priority indicated by our Lord's mandate that we "seek first the Kingdom of Heaven." Nothing else in Judah's national life, Hezekiah believed, would be correctly ordered if anything but the interests of God were put in first place. What was first must emphatically be put *there*, not second or somewhere else down the line.

This priority of God's Kingdom, for Hezekiah, involved more than the cleansing of the temple and the restoration of its worship. It also meant the renewal of spiritual wisdom, which explains the new king's interest in preserving Israel's ancient Wisdom literature (Proverbs 25:1). Such a pursuit of wisdom also had to do with the priority of the Kingdom of Heaven.

To Hezekiah, however, the "first-ness" of God's Kingdom was not a mere matter of sequence but a point of principle. The quest of the Kingdom was *first*, not only in the sense that it preceded everything else, but also in the sense that it laid the basis for everything else.

The foundation of an edifice, after all, is put down prior to the rest of the edifice, not simply because that is the usual and accepted order. It is the usual and accepted order because it is the *only conceivable* order. Indeed, the foundation of something belongs, in this sense, to a *different* order, because the rest of the thing is impossible without that foundation. It is the basis that supports the whole enterprise.

And this is what is meant by the priority of a principle. Such priority is more than mere succession—of getting things in the correct order. What is first pertains to an entirely other order—the order of principle. This is so plain a fact that it should not even have to be mentioned. Yet, Jesus did mention it, recognizing that some folks tend not to notice the obvious.

Just as that man is thought insane who imagines that he can first build a house and then lay its foundation, so is he insane who pretends to arrange a well-ordered life and then later starts on the foundation of it. Seeking God's Kingdom is the real foundation of the well-ordered life, and the Lord warns against building on any other.

❧ SIRACH 49 ☙

In the present chapter Sirach continues the history of Israel through the seventh and sixth centuries (vv. 1–13) and then jumps back to treat of the earlier patriarchs, who had been skipped (vv. 14–16).

The only praiseworthy king in the seventh century was Josiah (vv. 1–3), the great reformer who governed at Jerusalem between 640 BC and his death at the Battle of Megiddo in 609. Like the authors of Kingdoms and Chronicles, Sirach especially recalls Josiah's efforts to purge the land of idolatry (v. 2). Sirach does not mention the discovery of the Deuteronomic Code in the temple in 622 (4 Kingdoms 22:3–13; 2 Chronicles 34:14–21), but he does speak of the difficulty of Josiah's task in what he calls "days of lawlessness" (v. 3).

Josiah alone was numbered with David and Hezekiah among the kings worthy of honorable remembrance (v. 4). The history of Judah's other kings was full of disaster. In this assessment, it must be said, Sirach was more severe than the author of Kingdoms, who gave qualified approval to Asa, Jehoshaphat, and Jehoash.

The prophet chiefly associated with the reign of Josiah was, of course, Jeremiah, whose ministry extended even past the destruction of Jerusalem in 587 (v. 7). It is in connection with this tragedy that Sirach remembered Jeremiah (vv. 5–6).

Josiah and Jeremiah were tragic figures, good men overtaken by the accumulation of public sin over many decades. By the time they appeared on the scene in the second half of the seventh century, the course of evil had already run too far, and there was no preventing its final outcome. This was the assessment made by their contemporary, the prophetess Huldah (4 Kingdoms 22:14–20; 2 Chronicles 34:22–28).

It was the distinctive merit of Josiah and Jeremiah that they were very good men in very bad times. It is not surprising, therefore, that irony—and even a measure of absurdity—marked the circumstances of their passing: Josiah died prematurely as he attempted to assist the Babylonians against the Egyptians, and in less than two decades those Babylonians would destroy Jerusalem. After that destruction, the prophet Jeremiah was kidnapped into Egypt, where he ended his days in that very place from which Moses had led out the people of the Exodus.

To their contemporaries, both Josiah and Jeremiah doubtless appeared as failures. Their superior moral worth, however—their true greatness—was not lost on the inspired authors of the Holy Scriptures.

After the fall of Jerusalem in 587, Sirach moves more quickly to cover the Babylonian Exile (vv. 8–9) and its aftermath (vv. 11–13), barely mentioning the twelve minor prophets (v. 10), and then glances back briefly to recall more ancient figures in biblical history (vv. 14–16).

Ezekiel, the chief prophet during the Exile, he remembers as a visionary (v. 8), which, one supposes, is how most people *would* remember Ezekiel. It was apparently his vision of the dry bones that prompted Sirach's immediate prayer that God would "revive the bones / Of the twelve prophets from their place" (v. 10).

The aftermath of the Exile, in the eyes of Sirach, was dominated by two figures: the royal governor Zerubbabel and the high priest Jeshua, who were charged with the reconstruction of the second temple, finished in 515 (vv. 11–12). These men thus restored Israel's worship to the pinnacle of national life, against great odds and in very difficult times. Their contribution to Israel's history was essential to Sirach's thesis that God's eternal wisdom dwelt in that temple.

To those two figures—Zerubbabel and Jeshua—Sirach adds the name of Nehemiah, who reconstructed the walls of Jerusalem a century or so later (*circa* 445–425).

We might have expected two more names in this chapter: Daniel, who prophesied during the Babylonian Exile, and Ezra the Scribe, who contributed so much to the spiritual recovery of those who returned from the Exile.

In the case of Daniel, Sirach's failure to mention him is surely to be accounted for by the supposition that the Book of Daniel had not yet been written. Indeed, this supposition is consonant with the fact that that book was not included among the prophetic books of the Hebrew Bible. That is to say, the Book of Daniel was written too late to be included in that collection; this is the reason that it is found in the third part of the Hebrew Bible, the *Ketubim*, or "Writings."

In the case of Ezra, the reason for his omission is not so easy to discern, especially because he so clearly exemplified Sirach's ideals of the scribal vocation (chapter 39). This omission has yet to be adequately explained.

Equally puzzling is Sirach's sudden return to the Book of Genesis in order to call forth certain patriarchal figures of old: Enoch, Joseph, Shem, Seth, and even Adam (vv. 14–16). This unexpected addition has been accounted for in several ways, with varying degrees of plausibility. The most probable case is based on the supposition that Sirach, as he drew near the end of his orderly list of famous men, became aware that he had omitted these more ancient figures and determined to include them.

If this explanation is accepted, Sirach's inclusion resembles that of St. Luke, who followed an orderly geographical list of the nations represented on Pentecost morning, starting with the Persians in the east and proceeding to the Romans in the west. Having done this, Luke realized that he had omitted the people of Crete and Arabia, so he simply attached them at the end of his list (Acts 2:9–11).

Moreover, because of Sirach's inclusion of Enoch in this place, we suspect that he forgot that he had already written of Enoch in chapter 44.

Whatever the correct explanation of this break in sequence, Sirach ends his review of biblical history with Adam, where history itself began. Now he is ready to describe an imposing figure from his own lifetime in the next chapter.

❦ SIRACH 50 ❧

Now we come to the final and climactic figure in Sirach's long account, the otherwise obscure high priest, Simon II, to whose description he devotes almost this whole chapter.

The high priest Simon II did not leave a big mark on Jewish history. In fact, his death in 198 BC was the sole occasion of Simon's career that the historian of the Jews, Flavius Josephus, bothered to mention, and this only in passing (*Antiquities* 12.4.10). Simon was less prominent than his father, Onias II (12.4.1), and a great deal less significant than either of his two sons, Onias III (2 Maccabees 3—4; Antiquities 12.4.11) and Jason (2 Maccabees 4—5). In short, as the world normally appraises historical importance, Simon was not an important man. This fact renders more remarkable the high esteem in which Simon was held by Sirach, who wrote this eulogy of the high priest not long after his death.

And what was it about Simon that Sirach found so impressive? His solicitude for the divine worship, his refurbishing of the temple, his care for its appointments, and the personal dignity with which he enhanced the solemnity of its rituals.

The reverent grandeur of Israel's liturgical worship was of great moment to Sirach. Earlier in his historical panegyric he had paid detailed attention to the vestments and accoutrements of the Aaronic priesthood and its rites of sacrifice (45:6–17), in which he savored the mystic compound of holiness, beauty, and devotion. It was in the temple ministry of Simon, however, that Ben Sirach supremely discerned what it meant to "worship the Lord in the beauty of holiness."

It was chiefly in the temple at Jerusalem, Sirach believed, that God caused wisdom to dwell in this world. To "worship the Lord in the beauty of holiness" requires, first of all, holiness, and in this respect Simon the high priest was a model. Indeed, according to Ben Sirach, "when he went up to the holy altar, he made the garment of holiness honorable" (50:11, my translation).

This holiness of worship is clothed in beauty, and beauty is simply truth as lovable, truth discerned in its loveliness. The perception of truth is the discernment of form, nor is there beauty apart from form.

This is why biblical worship is formal, structured, patterned on a determined model. With respect to the form of worship, Moses on the mountain was told to make all things according to the heavenly pattern he beheld. This sane prescription would safeguard Israel from the worship of Canaanite gods and from silly Philistine heresies like that which thinks "beauty is in the eye of the beholder." Because every form of truth is heavenly and eternal, true liturgy is not simply old; it is necessarily timeless.

Sirach, in his account of Simon, has left us the Bible's finest description of Israel's worship. He gloried in the high praise of God according to the forms that God Himself prescribed. His eyes beheld the fire, the precious stones and beaten gold, the beauty of stately shapes and extravagant colors in vestments and sacred vessels. The air he breathed was laden with the richness of incense and aromatic oils, and his ears were filled with the silver trumpets and the chanting of the worshippers. He contemplated in the rituals of the temple the culminating adornment of creation itself.

In Sirach's estimation, then, Simon's task was not to make his mark on history, as the world regards history, but to serve in the dignified and solemn worship that transcends and sanctifies the events of men.

A benediction (vv. 22–24) follows the description of Simon's service of the Atonement, a fitting completion to Sirach's treatment of Simon. This benediction may be the content of the blessing (*evlogia*) mentioned in verse 21.

This blessing is paired with what may almost be called a curse (vv. 25–26). In the context this reference to three unfavored peoples may seem out of context, causing at least one interpreter (Father Daniel Harrington) to regard it as "a stray note" that "has no relationship to what precedes or follows it." It is possible, nonetheless, that "the vivid picture of sacrifice [we just had in the section on Simon the High Priest] suggested to the author the liturgical and religious rivalry between the Samaritans and the Jews" (Father Thomas Weber).

Whatever the explanation of its insertion here, something must be said of Sirach's sudden denunciation of Judea's near neighbors: the Idumeans, the Greeks, and the Samaritans.

First, however, there is a textual problem. As these verses now stand in the received text of the Septuagint, Sirach really mentions only two peoples, because those "who reside on the mountain of Samaria" are identical with "the foolish people who dwell in Shechem"—namely, the Samaritans. Following a Hebrew variant of this passage, however, we should read "Mount Seir" instead of "mountain of Samaria."

Interpreted thus, this is a reference to the Idumeans, descendants of the ancient Edomites that dwelt in the mountain ranges south and east of the Dead Sea. These Idumeans, displaced by migration of the Nabateans in the fourth century before Christ, had begun to encroach on the southern border of Judea, even as close as Hebron. We find them the consistent enemies of the Jews in several parts of 1 Maccabees. Somewhat later than Sirach's time, they were subjugated by John Hyrcanus (134–104). From that point on, the Idumeans were simply assimilated into Judaism. One of them, named Herod, even became a king of the Jews in the following century.

The second reference is to the Greeks, who heavily populated the cities of Philistia. The ancient Philistines were, in fact, of Greek and Cretan descent. We have had occasion to observe Sirach's sustained critique of Hellenic culture all through this book.

The third reference is to the Samaritans, whose temple was the pretentious rival to that in Jerusalem (John 4:20). Because they were of mixed blood, Sirach even declines to identify them as a "nation" (*ethnos*, v. 25). He calls them "the foolish people" (*ho laos ho moros*, v. 26).

Sirach finishes this chapter with a signature, as it were (v. 27), pronouncing a blessing on all those who live according to his instructions (vv. 28–29). We ourselves, if we so live, are the beneficiaries of this blessing. Sirach thus becomes the intercessor for those who study and apply his teaching. He remains, therefore, a holy teacher of the Church—traditionally called *Ecclesiasticus*, "the churchman"—to the end of time.

This chapter, a sort of appendix, comprises two poems. In view of Sirach's "sign off" at the end of the previous chapter, many readers suspect that he is the author of neither poem. Moreover, the second of these, preserved in Hebrew, is found among the Dead Sea Scrolls, independent of Sirach. Although it is impossible to be certain about the authorship of either poem, we must admit that the second is a good summary of the whole book.

In the first poem the author praises and thanks God for his deliverance from false accusers, who nearly had him killed (vv. 1–12). Although it is difficult to reconstruct the circumstances of this incident with precision, one feature is especially worthy of note: The poet had been accused to the "king" (v. 6). On the reasonable assumption that this poem is roughly contemporary with Sirach, the only king over Judea at that time was the Seleucid monarch at Antioch.

Now in fact we know that this throne received various accusations against, and complaints about, sundry individuals in Judea during the second century before Christ (for example, cf. 1 Maccabees 2:31; 3:26–27; 6:8, 28, 57; 7:5–25; 10:22). Whatever the specific circumstances of this poem, then, the denunciation of the author to the king fits a pattern well documented at that period.

One further feature of this first poem is also worthy of note—namely, its reference to "the Lord, the Father of my Lord" (v. 10). This expression is difficult to explain in the context of Sirach's time. Its closest biblical parallel is the opening line of Psalm 109 (110): "The Lord said to my Lord," which in its historical context referred to God speaking to the Davidic king (cf. the Christian sense of this line in Hebrews 1:13; Matthew 22:44; and multiple other New Testament texts). Such a sense is not possible here, because Judea no longer had its own king.

So who is this "Lord, the Father of my Lord"? It seems quite impossible to make sense of this reading except in a Christian context, in which God is identified in terms of Father and Son. This is a good occasion to remind ourselves that all extant Greek manuscripts of Sirach were copied by Christian hands.

The second poem is an alphabetical psalm (but only in Hebrew) about the pursuit of wisdom (vv. 13–30). As I mentioned above, it forms a kind of summary of the whole book.

ABOUT THE AUTHOR

Patrick Henry Reardon is pastor of All Saints Antiochian Orthodox Church in Chicago, Illinois, and Senior Editor of *Touchstone: A Journal of Mere Christianity.*

ANCIENT FAITH RADIO
www.ancientfaithradio.com

Visit www.ancientfaithradio.com to listen to podcasts by Patrick Henry Reardon.

ALSO BY PATRICK HENRY REARDON

Books in the *Orthodox Christian Reflections* series:

The Trial of Job:
Orthodox Christian Reflections on the Book of Job

"The Book of Job always constituted essential and formative reading about the ways of the soul. This has always been the conviction of the spiritual classics through the centuries. Yet, for some reason, the figure of Job is elusive to us— possibly because he seems so comfortably distant; or perhaps because he seems so frightfully close. What Fr. Patrick Reardon achieves with this book is to render Job comprehensible (to those of us who are still lay readers of Scripture), tangible (to those who have not yet tasted the way of darkness and despair), and accessible (to those who have already experienced any form of brokenness and broken-heartedness). Ultimately, all of us identify with one or another aspect of Job's life. As life inevitably informs and as this book intuitively confirms, one cannot sing Psalms without having read Job!"—Fr. John Chryssavgis, Author of *Light Through Darkness* and *Soul Mending*

Paperback, 112 pages (ISBN 978-1-888212-72-3) Order No. 006812—$10.95*

Creation and the Patriarchal Histories:
Orthodox Christian Reflections on the Book of Genesis

The Book of Genesis is foundational reading for the Christian, concerned as it is with the origins of our race and the beginnings of salvation history. Its opening pages provide the theological suppositions of the entire biblical story: Creation, especially that of man in God's image, the structure of time, man's relationship to God, the entrance of sin into the world, and God's selection of a specific line of revelation that will give structure to history. Early Christian writers such as St. Paul saw no dichotomy between the writings of the Law, of which Genesis is the beginning, and the Gospel. Rather, the Gospel is the key to understanding the Law. In *Creation and the Patriarchal Histories*, Fr. Reardon shows clearly how the proper understanding of Creation and the Fall informs all of Christian doctrine, and how the narratives of the patriarchs from Noah to Joseph pave the way for the salvation history that continues in Exodus.

Paperback, 160 pages (ISBN: 978-1-888212-96-9) CP Order No. 007605—$13.95*

Chronicles of History and Worship:
Orthodox Christian Reflections on the Books of Chronicles

The Old Testament Books of Chronicles contain some of the most neglected passages in all of Scripture. Understanding their message can be a difficult and daunting task for the modern reader. Popular writer and Old Testament scholar Patrick Reardon brings these important books to life, unfolding their powerful message for our own day and age.

Like any family history, the story of Chronicles is told with a distinct purpose in mind. It asks the question: "What was the real and lasting significance of King David and his house?" Beginning with the long list of names of the first chapter, this heritage is revealed in cosmic significance. It has in fact become the family tree of every true believer. The centrality of worship is also clearly revealed in these pages. The life pleasing to God is shown to be the life centered on the true worship that God has revealed to the world in the family history of His people. Far from being irrelevant or antiquated, these truths are alive today, reflected in the liturgy and life of the Church.

Paperback, 188 pages (ISBN: 978-1-888212-83-9) Order No. 007109—$14.95*

Other Books:
Christ in the Psalms

A highly inspirational book of meditations on the Psalms by one of the most insightful and challenging Orthodox writers of our day. Avoiding both syrupy sentimentality and arid scholasticism, *Christ in the Psalms* takes the reader on a thought-provoking and enlightening pilgrimage through this beloved "Prayer Book" of the Church.

Which psalms were quoted most frequently in the New Testament, and how were they interpreted? How has the Church historically understood and utilized the various psalms in her liturgical life? How can we perceive the image of Christ shining through the psalms? Lively and highly devotional, thought-provoking yet warm and practical, *Christ in the Psalms* sheds a world of insight upon each psalm, and offers practical advice for how to make the Psalter a part of our daily lives.

Paperback, 328 pages (ISBN 978-1-888212-21-7) Order No. 004927—$17.95*

Christ in His Saints

In this sequel to *Christ in the Psalms,* Patrick Henry Reardon once again applies his keen intellect to a topic he loves most dearly. Here he examines the lives of almost one hundred and fifty saints and heroes from the Scriptures—everyone from Abigail to Zephaniah, Adam to St. John the Theologian. This well-researched work is a veritable cornucopia of Bible personalities: Old Testament saints, New Testament saints, "Repentant saints," "Zealous saints," "Saints under pressure" . . . they're all here, and their stories are both fascinating and uplifting.

But *Christ in His Saints* is far more than just a biblical who's who. These men and women represent that ancient family into which, by baptism, all believers have been incorporated. Together they compose that great "cloud of witnesses" cheering us on and inspiring us through word and deed.

Paperback, 320 pages (ISBN 978-1-888212-68-6) Order No. 006538—$17.95*

*plus applicable tax and postage & handling charges. Prices current as of June, 2009. For complete ordering information, please log on to www.conciliarpress.com or call Conciliar Press at 800-967-7377.